Marriage,
Divorce, and
Remarriage

Kenneth E. Hagin

Unless otherwise indicated, all Scripture quotations are taken from the *King James Version* of the Bible.

14 13 12 11 10 09 08   10 09 08 07 06 05 04

Marriage Divorce & Remarriage
ISBN-13: 978-0-89276-536-2
ISBN-10: 0-89276-536-4
(Paperback)

In the U.S. write:
Kenneth Hagin Ministries
P.O. Box 50126
Tulsa, OK 74150-0126
1-888-28-FAITH
www.rhema.org

In Canada write:
Kenneth Hagin Ministries
P.O. Box 335, Station D
Etobicoke (Toronto), Ontario
Canada, M9A 4X3
1-866-70-RHEMA
www.rhemacanada.org

Marriage, DIVORCE & Remarriage

Kenneth E. Hagin

CONTENTS

Introduction

I n the day and age that we live, it is imperative that our families are strong and secure. The two institutions that the devil fights harder than anything else are the family and the Church. So it is important to understand what the Word of God says concerning the family.

God wants your marriage to be successful and your family to be a place of love. Whether married or single, God wants your life to be peaceful. By coming in line with the Word, you will experience good results. You will see your home become like Heaven on earth!

This book is divided into six chapters. Chapter 1 focuses on some common misunderstandings people have had concerning what the Bible says about marriage, divorce, and remarriage. You see, what Jesus said in Matthew chapter 19 and what Paul said in First Corinthians chapter 7 seem to conflict. And for years, people have struggled to find the answer. I explain in Chapter 2 how to interpret these passages based on commonly accepted rules of Bible interpretation.

Then I explain in Chapter 3 the law that is to govern the Body of Christ today—the law of love. Whatever situation you find yourself in—whether married to a Christian, married to an unbeliever, abandoned by a Christian, abandoned by an unsaved spouse, or single—you can pick up where you are and walk on in the love of God.

Chapter 4 goes into detail concerning God's ideal of marriage. From the time Adam sinned until Jesus Christ came to redeem mankind, man was never able to have the divine type of marriage that God had planned in the Garden of Eden. The life and nature of God was not in mankind at this time. But today as men and women under the New Covenant, we are able to fulfill God's ideal for marriage. In this Chapter, I discuss the area of submission and authority, specifically in a marriage relationship, because of an error that has been perpetuated in the Body of Christ. I explain what it means to submit one to another in a marriage relationship.

For more than sixty-five years, I have listened to the problems that people face in their marriages and families. I have discovered that all marital problems center around four things. In Chapter 5, I discuss these four areas at length and offer practical solutions for overcoming any problems in these areas.

Chapter 6 focuses on the family. By your actions and your words, you create the atmosphere in your home. When you set a good example for your children and surround them with faith and love, you are providing the right resources that will enable them to grow up to be godly men and women.

Whether you are single, married, or divorced, this book is intended to help you fulfill God's ideal for your home.

You can have the marriage you desire. You can have the family you desire. By simply understanding what the Word of God says and then acting on the Word, you can experience the love and peace of God in your home.

CHAPTER ONE

Marriage, Divorce, and Remarriage

B ecause of the need of the hour, the conditions of the day, and the position of the Church, it's imperative that we address the subject of marriage, divorce, and remarriage. This is the greatest problem of human relationships. Divorce and remarriage has become a national issue.

There are three main perspectives from which I write this book. First, I am writing as one who knows the pain of a broken home. My father abandoned the family when I was five years old. I know what it is to grow up without a father. I've seen the pain and pressure put upon a single mother trying to raise a family of her own. My own mother suffered horribly, even to the point of an emotional breakdown and numerous suicide attempts.

I know the injury that divorce can inflict in a young heart. My brother and I hated our father for what he did and even planned to kill him when we got old enough. I can certainly understand why God said He hates divorce (Mal. 2:14–16) because I've seen and experienced the heartache and devastation it causes.

Second, I also write as one who knows the joys of a wonderful marriage. At the time of this writing, I have been married for sixty-two years. I've seen the blessedness of a marriage in which the love of God rules. I've known the benefits of having a godly partner, a sweetheart with whom I've been able to walk through life, sharing its blessings and challenges together. We have faced difficulties in life and in marriage, just like every other couple, but God has seen us through. We've never looked for an easy way out of marriage; we've always looked for God to help us, and He has.

Third, I write as a minister of the Gospel, as one who is divinely commissioned to keep the Word of God as the supreme guide and authority in all things. I have seen the pain, anguish, and condemnation that has been placed upon victims of divorce as a result of misinterpretations of Scripture, legalistic beliefs, and "religious" thinking. I have seen those who felt they were representing Christ as they denounced people who had been divorced and remarried, treating them as "second-class Christians" or as though they had committed the unpardonable sin. However, they were unlike Christ in the mercy and grace with which He ministered to people.

On the other hand, I have seen some couples who claim to be Christian, but treated their marriage as an "easy-come, easy-go" proposition. I am not advocating this attitude of "looseness," the lack of consecration, that seems to be held by so many in church circles today.

Our problem is that we have been raised in different churches that taught different things, and we haven't done any thinking for ourselves. We have just accepted what others have said. But I have always been a little bit different. I was born and raised Southern Baptist, but in 1934, I received light on the subject of divine healing on the bed of sickness, and I saw that the Bible taught something my church at the time didn't teach.

So from that day until this, I've never been one to follow church teaching without studying for myself, because following church teaching almost sent me to the grave.

When I was on the bed of sickness as a teenage boy, my pastor offered me no hope. He didn't know about faith and healing. He told me, "Just be patient, my boy; in a few more days, it will all be over."

As a young minister, I didn't give much thought to the subject of marriage, divorce, and remarriage. I had no reason to give much thought to it. But three different situations of marriage, divorce, and remarriage triggered something on the inside of me and started me thinking about the subject. Since then, I've spent hours, days, months, and years on this subject! Yet if I tried to interpret First Corinthians chapter 7 in the light of what Jesus said in Matthew chapter 19, I would become hopelessly confused. It seems that Paul contradicts Jesus by giving an "exception" that Jesus did not acknowledge. It was only after I saw some "real life" situations, though, that I had to come to terms with this seeming contradiction.

First Situation—Unfaithful Wife

I got saved on the bed of sickness at 15 years of age. I was healed right before my seventeenth birthday and started going out to minister. Those first two years, I just preached wherever the door opened: young people's groups, the street, jail services, and home prayer services.

Then when I was 18, I preached a meeting with another minister. We got many people saved in a certain community. They wanted to start a church and asked me to pastor it. I preached for six or seven weeks to decide whether or not I would pastor the church. I decided I would.

There was a young man in that town whom I'd known since I was a little boy. He was 10 years older than I was.

This man was an adopted child. Although his parents had raised about thirty-two different kids, he was the only one they adopted. They just raised the others.

Well, this young man's parents were good folks. They were church people, and I'm satisfied they were saved people. This young man was raised in church. He later said to me, "I really didn't know that I wasn't born again until I got around Full Gospel people, and I found out I was just a church member."

When he was about twenty-two years old, he married a woman there in town. At that time, I was only 12 years old, but in a little town of 8,500 people, nearly everyone knows everything that's happening, particularly things like this.

This young man made a living as a businessman. All the businesses of that day were right around the square. As a kid, I remember hearing the businessmen talk. They would say, "Why in the world did that fine Christian (they called him a Christian because he went to church) young man marry that woman? Doesn't he know what she is?" Actually, she was a prostitute.

In his sheltered life, he was very naive. This woman just latched onto him because she thought the family name would give her a little prestige. And so, they were married for four or five years.

During those years, almost everyone was talking about this young man behind his back and laughing at him, because this woman continued to see other men. And he, in his innocence, didn't seem to notice that anything was wrong. Finally, she left town and ran off with one of the men whom she had been seeing while she was married to this man. No one ever heard from her again.

This man's heart was broken. He would weep and weep. So some of the other businessmen began to talk to him and told him what his ex-wife had been doing. I was only a little kid at this time.

Then when I was 18 years of age and he was twenty-eight, he told me what his reaction was when the businessmen told him about his wife. He said, "Man, I could hardly believe it. I began to think back, and I could see they were right. I was just too naive. I didn't see anything."

After he divorced, he got saved in a Full Gospel church in town. According to the beliefs of this church, he (as a divorced person) could not remarry now that he was a Christian. Now if he had remarried *before* he got saved, this church would have accepted him.

I was just 18 at the time and hadn't really studied the subject of marriage and divorce, but on the inside of me, I knew these beliefs weren't right. I had learned to follow my spirit. Something on the inside of me told me that he should be able to remarry.

This man was not baptized in the Holy Ghost; he didn't speak with tongues. But he was saved and attended the Full Gospel church. He played the piano for the church.

In the meantime, a certain lady, his high-school sweetheart, moved back to his town. She had never married. Someone invited her to come to the Full Gospel church, and she got saved. The lady found out that she had been just a church member. She had never been born again. So she got saved. She was also a musician, so she would play the piano some, and then he would play the piano some. They swapped out. That was all we had in those days—just a piano. We didn't have an organ or anything else.

They started working together in music and spending time with each other. They rekindled their high-school courtship. Thinking nothing about it, they went to the pastor to ask him to marry them.

He said, "Oh, no! You can't do that. Both of you would go to hell!"

Well, I didn't think he was right, but I was not going to argue with the pastor. I had learned to respect my elders. And since I was still a young fellow and hadn't looked into the Scripture on the subject of marriage, divorce, and remarriage yet, I just kept my mouth shut.

Then the pastor who was opposed to their marriage left and another pastor took his position. Between the time that the former pastor accepted another church and the new pastor got there, there was an interim of several weeks when guest speakers filled in. And during this interim, the couple went away and got married.

When the new pastor got there, he didn't know a thing in the world about this couple. So they continued with their music. They continued teaching Sunday school classes. They never bothered anyone. They went right on with their work in the church. The new pastor stayed there for a while, and then God called him somewhere else. The former pastor was invited to come back to pastor the church, and he accepted.

By then, I was pastoring a little church in Tom Bean, Texas. Occasionally, I would go back to this Full Gospel church to visit. One day the pastor said to me, "You know, they're married."

I said, "Yeah, I know it."

He said, "The church is only a few years old and, rather than cause a split, I'm just going to leave it alone." He thought they were wrong and that they were going to hell when they died. But he didn't want to cause a split in the church.

Well, I was busy. I didn't do much thinking about the subject. I was twenty, almost twenty-one years old. I was not greatly concerned about the subject, not even particularly concerned about marriage, much less divorce and remarriage. I was busy serving God.

Later, I went back down there to visit, and I noticed that the pastor had a worried look on his face. I could tell that there was something bothering him. It was very easy to tell.

"What's wrong?" I asked.

"Well," he said, "I don't understand it."

I said, "What don't you understand?"

He said, "Do you remember the couple in my church who married after the man had been divorced? He had been divorced, and she had never married. Then they married one another." I just stayed quiet about the whole thing, because I didn't want to split the church in two.

"Well," he continued, "this couple was attending a revival meeting, and both of them received the baptism in the Holy Ghost while living in adultery!"

I said, "They did?"

"Yeah," he said, "my wife was praying with her in the altar when she was filled with the Holy Spirit and began to speak in tongues. And I was praying with him in the altar. He received the same Holy Spirit, and I heard him speak in other tongues. But I can't figure it out. Why would God baptize them with the Holy Ghost when they're living in adultery? I've been trying to figure it out."

Well, as I said, I did a lot of thinking on my own, but I kept my mouth shut. I had learned to respect my elders.

I said to him, "Did you ever figure it out?"

He said, "The only way I can figure it out (and you know it must have been him 'figuring it out,' not the Lord telling him) is that God knows that they're going to hell, anyway, when they die. So He's just blessing them all He can in this life."

I never said a word, but that got me thinking! I thought to myself, *Now, that's stupid.*

When I left that parsonage, I said to myself, *I'm going to look into that subject. I don't know what the Bible says on the subject, because I haven't really examined it. But I'm going to look into it.*

Second Situation—Wife Leaves

Another situation that I knew of also motivated me to study the subject of marriage, divorce, and remarriage. A pastor, a minister of the Gospel, was left with five children when his wife ran off with another man. She had done that twice before, and he took her back. I think he did so just for the children's sake. But she finally left and didn't want to come back. So this pastor was left with five children.

The oldest child was probably 12 years old, and the youngest one was about 18 months old. As long as he didn't remarry, he would be accepted and could still pastor in his denomination. But a man who is between the ages of 35 and 40 and has 5 children needs a wife. Those children needed a mother. So he remarried. And because he did, he was forced to give up the church that he was pastoring. He was with a Full Gospel denomination, but he had to surrender his certificate of fellowship. He was no longer in fellowship with the other brethren.

What could the man do? God had called him to preach. Well, he started having services in a high-school auditorium. People started coming, and it wasn't long until he had hundreds of people. It wasn't very long until he had one of the largest churches in the city.

Most of the Full Gospel preachers were criticizing him. They were saying, "How can God bless him? He's living in adultery."

A pastor of the same Full Gospel denomination said to me, "After his wife left for the third time and ran off with that fellow, I went by to help him if I could. His car was in the driveway. I knocked on the front door, and no one answered. The children were in school, except for the one who was 18 months old. I knew he must be there, because his car was sitting in the driveway. So I walked around to the back. I saw him on the back porch with that little one in his arms, just weeping."

This pastor said to me, "I never could criticize him. I knew those children needed a mother. He needed a wife. I didn't understand it. It didn't necessarily agree with the teaching I had received, but I was not going to criticize him."

Soon after, we had a Full Gospel Bible conference. The head man in our state was preaching. In his sermon he referred to this pastor who had remarried. He didn't call the man's name, but we all knew whom he was talking about. When this two-day Bible conference was over, some of my church members asked me about it, because they had heard others talking about it. So I repeated what the head man in our state said.

The members of my church asked me, "Well, what do you think about it?"

I said, "I'm a young man. I just go along with the elders." Then I thought no more about it.

That weekend, my father-in-law and mother-in-law came down to visit my wife and me, and after the Sunday night service, my wife and two children went home with them. I was going up to my in-laws after Wednesday night's service.

So I was in the parsonage by myself while my wife and two children were at my in-law's house. At 10:15 p.m., I reached up and turned the light out. Back in the 1940s, the light hung down in the middle of the room.

Then I knelt by the head of the bed, because I was going to get right into bed. Well, it was very dark in the room when I turned the light out. With my eyes wide open, I still was not able to see a thing. So I knelt down and started to pray. I hadn't said but a word or two when my whole room lit up, brighter than it had been with the light on.

I could see every piece of furniture in the room. It was brighter than the noonday sun! The whole room lit up, and I heard a voice say, "Who art thou that criticizes another man's servant?"

I said, "Lord, uh, I didn't criticize Your servant."

The Lord said, "Didn't you say such-and-such about Brother _____?" The Lord called him "brother."

"No," I said, "I really didn't say that. I was quoting Brother _____. I was repeating what he said."

"Well," the Lord said, "when you repeated what he said, that was tantamount to you saying it."

In my defense I said, "Lord, You know, I thought he shouldn't have remarried."

The Lord didn't say one word about that. He said again, "Who art thou that criticizes another man's servant?"

I said, "Lord, isn't he wrong? I mean, that's what Brother _____ is saying, and that's what our church teaches."

He said, "Who art thou that criticizes another man's servant?" He didn't even answer the question. Then He asked, "Is he your servant or My servant?"

I answered, "If he's anyone's servant, he's Yours. He's definitely not mine!"

"If he is My servant, then who are you to criticize another man's servant? If he's My servant, I'm able to make him stand, and I will make him stand." (The Lord was really just correcting me based on what the Bible says in Romans 14:4.)

I said, "Lord, forgive me. I was wrong." Then the light went out. From that day until this, I've kept my mouth shut. But that incident started me thinking about the subject of marriage, divorce, and remarriage. I began to study the Word of God on the subject a little more. Then I began to ask questions. I asked certain leaders of the denomination what Paul meant in First Corinthians chapter 7.

They would say, "We don't know."

I would say, "Well, we *ought* to know."

I couldn't find a preacher or a minister that could explain First Corinthians chapter 7 to me. And I talked to the leading Bible teachers of that day. But not one of them could explain it to me. Every one of them would back off and say, "I don't know."

I thought, *Well, why don't we know?* So I got into the Word again concerning marriage, divorce, and remarriage. I didn't have time just to study this one subject all the time. I had to preach a sermon Sunday morning, Sunday night, and Wednesday night. I had to study in other areas and do other things as well. But in my spare moments, I would study this subject.

Third Situation—Husband Leaves

Then a third incident happened that triggered me to really search out the answer. My only sister's husband left her. Now I had talked to him. I knew, of course, that he was running around with other women, gambling, drinking, and so on. But he had a family to take care of.

After he left my sister for another woman, I was preaching in west Texas, and God spoke to me. I drove more than

300 miles. There were no freeways in those days. I drove all night long, and then I located him.

He was a salesman. As he was coming out of a place of business, I said, "Doc, I want to talk to you." I spoke to him kindly and with tears, "The Lord sent me down here; He spoke to me." He began to cry. He cried more than I did. Tears were running out of his eyes like water running out of a faucet.

He said, "I believe it. I know you. I've followed you for years. I believe what you're saying."

I said, "The Lord spoke to me and told me to come and talk to you."

I talked to him about being saved. He said, "You're right. I know you're right, but I'm not going to do it."

I said, "All right, Doc, let me approach you from another standpoint then. If you don't want to be a Christian, if you don't want to serve God, at least make a change for the sake of your children. Think about your little boys. I came from a broken home. I know the misery. I know what happened to me. People spit on, kicked, and knocked me around. I was mad at the whole world."

He said, "I know you're right, but I'm not going to do anything about it."

I said, "Doc, if you can't be a Christian, at least for the sake of your children, show some decency and respect. At least be a decent human being. At least be a man. Don't run around with every woman in the country."

He jumped! He jumped like I had hit him with a whip. He then wept and sobbed, saying, "I know you're right. I'm just a dog, but I'm going to stay that way. I want it that way."

Then I said, "I've done my best. I've done what God told me to do." He went away weeping. I went back to my meeting.

Between three and four o'clock in the morning, I was lying on the floor in the church auditorium, praying for him.

The Spirit of God said, "Get up from here."

I got up and said, "Why?"

He said, "Don't pray for him anymore."

"Lord," I said, "he's lost. He's going to hell."

The Lord said, "I know it."

"Well, what do you mean, 'Don't pray for him'?"

"He's joined to his idols. Did you ever read in the Old Testament where I finally said, 'Leave Ephraim alone'? [See Hosea 4:17.] Don't you ever, the longest day you live, pray another prayer for him, because he's going to die and go to hell."

How does God know? I believe He knows the future better than we know the past. I understand that Doc, my ex-brother-in-law, died at an early age cursing God.

Now my sister was left with five children. She had to go to work to make a living for them. Even though Doc was supposed to help her, he never did pay anything to help support his own children.

I helped them all I could. I did a lot for them, until eventually my sister met a gentleman, and they got married. According to the teaching of my church, you know, she was not supposed to remarry. The church believed that she was living in adultery.

Well, they got married about Christmastime. They came over to visit us. Between Christmas and New Year's Day, they were with us in our services. On the first Sunday of the new year, I preached. My sister had been in church at one time, but because of all the difficulties she had encountered, she had gotten out of church and wasn't going. She was in a low state of spiritual fellowship.

Now I've only seen this manifestation three times in my sixty-five years of ministry. About the time I was finishing my sermon, suddenly a light flashed. Now the buildings were well lit, but it was just like a giant flash bulb went off and everyone was temporarily blinded. No one could tell what happened because no one could see anything. In other words, it happened just as fast as I can snap my finger. Suddenly there were four or five people in the altar. How did they get there? We never did figure that out.

My sister was sitting in the third pew. She wasn't next to the aisle; she was in the middle of the pew. Now if someone comes out of a pew, they're bound to brush against your knees. You would know if someone came by you. But it happened so fast. And my sister was one of the people who was immediately down at the altar. She had never been filled with the Holy Spirit and spoken in other tongues. But when I saw her at the altar, she was speaking in other tongues. Not only did the Lord restore her to fellowship, He also filled her with the Holy Spirit.

According to the church, she shouldn't have been able to be filled with the Holy Spirit and speak in other tongues. According to the church, the Lord shouldn't have baptized her with the Holy Spirit. According to the church, she was living in adultery. This really triggered me to study more on the subject of marriage, divorce, and remarriage. My sister came back to the Lord on the first day of 1946. It took me three years to find the answer, but I found it in 1949.

Who's Right?
Paul or Jesus?

I studied after the leading Bible teachers in Full Gospel groups and other groups as well to see what they had to say on the subject of marriage, divorce, and remarriage. Then I asked some leaders what they thought Paul meant by certain statements he made. I found out that they were just as confused as I was.

They would simply say, "Well, I just don't know." And some would say, "I would rather follow Jesus than Paul." I would wonder, *Who's right? Paul or Jesus?*

In 1957 I was preaching in California. I picked up the *Los Angeles Times* and noticed that a man who was the president of a seminary in the northeastern part of the United States was visiting Los Angeles. His picture was on the front page of the paper. So I thought he must be a man of importance. In the article, the news reporter inquired why this man had come to their city. The man responded by saying that it was partly business and partly just for pleasure.

While this man was in Los Angeles, he spoke at one of the seminaries there. He addressed the student body and the faculty. The *Los Angeles Times* covered his lecture on the whole back page of the first section of the newspaper. They covered his lecture thoroughly. Because I was interested, I read it very closely.

This man said in effect, "I'm going to revive an old argument. If you haven't had seminary training, you don't necessarily know this. But a war has been waged in theological circles for the last 400 years. It has been discussed on the level of higher education in seminaries and universities. The issue is 'Who's right? Paul or Jesus?'" What Paul said in First Corinthians chapter 7 seems to contradict with what Jesus said in Matthew chapter 19.

And so, this president of a seminary said, "Well, I'm prone to follow Jesus." Now that sounds real good; it sounds real religious. Of course, we should follow Jesus. But who's right? Since the Bible is inspired by the Holy Ghost, then both of them would have to be right.

Well, on the inside of me, the Holy Ghost spoke up and said, "Both of them *are* right. Jesus is referring to the commandment given to the Jews, and Paul is talking to the Church." Jesus was accurately interpreting the Law of Moses concerning marriage, divorce, and remarriage to the Jews. And Paul was accurately applying the law of love concerning marriage, divorce, and remarriage to the Church (see Matt. 19 and 1 Cor. 7).

There is the answer. It's very simple. The Holy Ghost is the Teacher. He will teach you. He will bring to your remembrance all things (John 14:26). I could see it so clearly when He spoke to me. And so, that's what the Holy Ghost said to me: "Jesus is talking to the Jews, and Paul is talking to the Church."

The Holy Ghost is trying to tell us things all the time, but our head is dominating us instead of our spirits, so we don't listen. One great lesson that we need to learn and take to heart is that we need to listen to the Holy Spirit. I see that to be a great imperfection or shortcoming among "faith" people or "Word" people. If we are not careful, we will forget about the Holy Spirit.

Rightly Dividing the Word of God

Another shortcoming among many believers is that they don't do much thinking or studying for themselves. Instead, they just follow what someone else said.

There are ministers who have taken texts out of context and made them say something that the Bible doesn't say. Anyone can prove anything he wants to prove by taking one verse or two verses out of a chapter and making them stand alone.

You can make the Bible say anything you want it to say. But when you read the entire context—the whole section of Scripture—then it throws more light on the subject. Paul gives us a clue about how to read the Bible in writing to Timothy, a young minister and spiritual son of Paul. Paul told Timothy in Second Timothy 2:15 to study. In order to study, you have to think, don't you? You know, you can read without thinking. You can read another man's thoughts. But to study, you have to think!

You've heard me say it before. I've said it for fifty years, and I'm going to keep on saying it. Don't accept something just because I said it or someone else said it. Study the Word of God for yourself and see if that's what the Word of God actually says. Then you're not following what Brother Hagin said or someone else said. You're following what God said. Don't follow what someone else said, anyway, because

17

preachers, just like everyone else, are at various stages of spiritual development. You might be following a baby Christian, even though you may have developed beyond that. Paul tells Timothy, a fellow minister of the Gospel of Jesus Christ, to diligently study to show himself approved unto God (2 Tim. 2:15).

If you take the reverse implication of that verse, a person who doesn't study is not approved. God doesn't approve a person who doesn't study. And he doesn't approve his ministry. That is why so many ministers wind up on the spiritual junk heap.

What does the rest of the verse say? *"Study to show thyself approved unto God, a workman that needeth not to be ashamed, RIGHTLY DIVIDING THE WORD OF TRUTH"* (2 Tim. 2:15). People often get in trouble because they don't rightly divide the Word of truth. Well, if it has to be divided *rightly*, then it can be divided *wrongly*.

When I first got saved and started in the ministry, I heard someone give this simple rule of Bible interpretation, and it registered on me. In studying the Bible, always ask yourself: "Who's doing the speaking?" "What are they speaking about?" "And to whom are they speaking?"

It's very easy to take some of the things that God said and say, "Well, now, *God* is saying this." But you have to look at whom God was talking to. Sometimes He was speaking to the Jews; and what He said didn't even apply to anyone else.

Let's look in First Corinthians where Paul is writing to the Church at Corinth.

1 CORINTHIANS 10:32

> 32 *Give none offence, neither to the Jews, nor to the Gentiles, nor to the church of God.*

Notice that there are three classes of people addressed in the Word of God: 1) the Jews, God's covenant people; 2) the

Church, God's own family; and 3) the Gentiles, heathen people (everyone who's not either in the Church or a Jew).

The Mosaic Law Was Given to the Jews

God gave the Mosaic Law about marriage and divorce to the Jew only. The Mosaic Law was never supposed to govern the nations that were around them or the Gentiles who lived among them.

Let's look at the Mosaic Law in Deuteronomy chapter 24.

DEUTERONOMY 24:1–4

1   *When a man hath taken a wife, and married her, and it come to pass that she find no favour in his eyes, because he hath found some uncleanness in her: then let him write her a bill of divorcement, and give it in her hand, and send her out of his house.*

2   *And when she is departed out of his house, she may go and be another man's wife.*

3   *And if the latter husband hate her, and write her a bill of divorcement, and giveth it in her hand, and sendeth her out of his house; or if the latter husband die, which took her to be his wife;*

4   *Her former husband, which sent her away, may not take her again to be his wife, after that she is defiled; for that is abomination before the Lord: and thou shalt not cause the land to sin, which the Lord thy God giveth thee for an inheritance.*

Under the Old Testament, a woman seldom had any voice in the choice of a husband. Her father sold her to the man who desired her. If she pleased the man, he kept her. If not, he had a legal right under the Mosaic Law to return her to her father for the purchase price.

In Matthew chapter 19, Jesus expounded the Mosaic Law about marriage and divorce to the Jews. He was speaking to the Jews. He was not giving the Gentiles the law that was to govern them. The Gentiles were not under the Mosaic Law—then or now. They have never been under it. And Jesus was not giving the Body of Christ the law to govern them. Jesus was simply answering the Pharisees' questions about the Mosaic Law.

Let's read Matthew chapter 19.

MATTHEW 19:1–3

1 *And it came to pass, that when Jesus had finished these sayings, he departed from Galilee, and came into the coasts of Judea beyond Jordan;*

2 *And great multitudes followed him; and he healed them there.*

3 *The Pharisees also came unto him, tempting him, and saying unto him, Is it lawful for a man to put away his wife FOR EVERY CAUSE?*

The Pharisees asked Jesus if it was lawful for a man to divorce his wife "for every cause" because they wanted to find out if Jesus agreed with the thinking that a person could divorce for a wide variety of reasons. You see, people had questions about what Moses meant when he talked about a man divorcing his wife after he found "some uncleanness" in her (see Deut. 24:1). One group thought that the term "some uncleanness" referred to a wide range of things. While another group thought that the term only referred to sexual immorality.

Let's continue reading.

MATTHEW 19:4–9

4 *And he answered and said unto them, Have ye not read, that he which made them at the beginning made them male and female,*

5 *And said, For this cause shall a man leave father and mother, and shall cleave to his wife: and they twain shall be one flesh?*

6 *Wherefore they are no more twain, but one flesh.*
What therefore God hath joined together, let not
man put asunder.

7 *They say unto him, Why did Moses then command*
to give a writing of divorcement, and to put her
away?

8 *He saith unto them, Moses because of the hardness*
of your hearts suffered you to put away your wives:
but from the beginning it was not so.

9 *And I say unto you, Whosoever shall put away his*
wife, except it be for the cause of fornication, and
shall marry another, committeth adultery: and
whoso marrieth her which is put away doth commit
adultery.

Jesus answered the Pharisees' question in Matthew 19:9.
He made it clear that Moses was specifically referring to fornication, or sexual sin.

However, in First Corinthians 7:15 and 16, Paul intro-
duced an "exception" that Jesus did not mention. Paul said
that if an unbelieving spouse decides to leave, the Christian
spouse is not under bondage to the marriage vows. This is
the seeming contradiction between Paul and Jesus. This is
what has caused so much confusion in the Body of Christ.

We must remember that Jesus was interpreting the Law
of Moses to the Jews, while Paul was showing how the law
of love applied to the Church. In Matthew chapter 19, Jesus
was specifically answering a question about what was lawful
(according to Moses). In First Corinthians chapter 7, Paul
was answering the question, "What would love do?" What
some have described as a contradiction is really no contradiction at all.

Then Jesus reminded the Pharisees of a better law than
that of Moses. In Matthew 19:6, Jesus repeats the statement
and commandment that God gave Adam at the beginning:
"*Wherefore they are no more twain, but one flesh. What therefore*

God hath joined together, let not man put asunder." In Old Testament times, it was not uncommon for a man to have a plurality of wives. Which one did he become one with? Man in his fallen state didn't have the love of God shed abroad in his heart. So, you see, until Jesus came to redeem mankind, no one could fulfill God's ideal for marriage because man, being dominated by the sin nature, didn't have the life of God. But two born-again believers, full of the love of God, can fulfill Matthew 19:6 and become one.

Then the Pharisees asked, "Why did Moses give them a *command* of divorce?" Jesus said that he *permitted* them to divorce due to the hardness of their hearts (see Matt. 19:8). But with born-again people, this shouldn't be so! A born-again person's heart has been made new.

In other words, from the time Adam sinned and fell until Jesus Christ came to redeem mankind, man was never able to have the divine type of marriage that God had planned in the Garden of Eden. Why? They were not born-again men through the New Birth, with the nature of God in them. Their hearts hadn't been changed. The Jews were natural men living under the Law, redeemed by the blood of bulls and goats. In Matthew 19:9, Jesus said to the Jew under the Law, "Whosoever puts his wife away except for fornication and shall marry another commits adultery." Jesus didn't say this to born-again believers!

Let's continue reading.

MATTHEW 19:10-11

10 *His disciples say unto him, If the case of the man be so with his wife, it is not good to marry.*

11 *But he said unto them, ALL MEN CANNOT RECEIVE THIS SAYING, SAVE THEY TO WHOM IT IS GIVEN.*

Notice the disciples said in verse 10 that it is not good to marry. Now this verse is not given to everyone—only to those to whom it's given! Jesus said unto them, "All men cannot receive this saying." I want you to notice that it's not a commandment or a law. Jesus calls it a "saying." All men cannot receive this saying. That's the key. It is only given to those who can receive it.

Let's read the next verse.

MATTHEW 19:12

12 *For there are some eunuchs, which were so born from their mother's womb: and there are some eunuchs, which were made eunuchs of men: and there be eunuchs, which have made themselves eunuchs for the kingdom of heaven's sake. HE THAT IS ABLE TO RECEIVE IT, LET HIM RECEIVE IT.*

In this sense, a eunuch is a castrated man—a man deprived of testes, or external genitals. Some men are born this way. Some are made this way by men. And others are made this way for the Kingdom of Heaven's sake.

Let's look at the *Williams* translation.

MATTHEW 19:10–12 (Williams)

10 *The disciples said to Him, "If that is a man's relation to his wife, there is no advantage in getting married."*

11 *He said to them, "IT IS NOT EVERY MAN WHO HAS THE CAPACITY TO CARRY OUT THIS SAYING, but it is for those to whom the capacity has been given.*

12 *For some are born incapable of marriage, and some have been made so by men, and some have made themselves so for the sake of the kingdom of heaven. Let him accept it who can."*

So Jesus is saying that if a man is incapable of marriage because he was born that way, made that way by men, or made so for the Kingdom of Heaven's sake, then it is good for him not to marry. You see, this saying is not for everyone. It is only for those who can accept it. Not everyone can.

In the Book of Romans, Paul explains how the Jew who has come into the Body of Christ no longer lives under the Law of Moses.

ROMANS 7:1–6

1   *Know ye not, brethren, for I speak to them that know the law, how that the law hath dominion over a man as long as he liveth?* [Paul is talking to people who know the Law of Moses.]

2   *For the woman which hath an husband is bound by the law* [of Moses] *to her husband so long as he liveth; but if the husband be dead, she is loosed from the law of her husband.*

3   *So then if, while her husband liveth, she be married to another man, she shall be called an adulteress: but if her husband be dead, she is free from that law; so that she is no adulteress, though she be married to another man.*

4   *Wherefore, MY BRETHREN, YE ALSO ARE BECOME DEAD TO THE LAW* [You have become dead to what he just finished saying.] *by the body of Christ; that ye should be married to another, even to him who is raised from the dead, that we should bring forth fruit unto God.*

5   *For when we were in the flesh, the motions of sins, which were by the law, did work in our members to bring forth fruit unto death.*

6   *But now WE ARE DELIVERED FROM THE LAW, that being dead wherein we were held; that we should serve in newness of spirit, and not in the oldness of the letter.*

Much suffering has come to innocent men and women who are uninformed. God only governs the marriages of His people! We have tried to put unsaved men and women under the Mosaic Law, but they are not. And the Church is not under the Mosaic Law, either.

Men are born again into the New Covenant. Those who haven't been born again, Jew or Gentile, are not in the Body of Christ, so they are not under the law of the New Covenant—the law of love. They couldn't keep it anyway. A person can't love another person like Christ did without having the love of Christ in him. And a person who has not been regenerated, or born again, doesn't have that love. The love of God must be shed abroad in a person's heart by the Holy Ghost (Rom. 5:5).

The Old Covenant was fulfilled in Jesus. So there is no Mosaic Law in force today. For a Jew to come under the law of the New Covenant, he must be born again. So neither Jew nor Gentile has any marriage or divorce law today, except the law of man. The Jew may try to keep the old Mosaic Law, but he cannot do it. He never could, and he never will (Acts 15:10). Christ arose and fulfilled the Law.

Since 72 A.D., there hasn't been a high priest, an altar, or an atonement sacrificed for the Jew. The Jew must be born again, just as the Gentile. The law of marriage and divorce given to Moses was given to the Jew only. To the Jew, it was enforced until Jesus came and fulfilled it. Jesus ended the reign of the Mosaic Law, even though Jews may still try to abide by the Law.

The Unsaved

Does the unsaved world have any law of marriage and divorce? Yes, the laws of men formulated by individual civil governments govern those who are unsaved. Is the unsaved world under the law of God? No, they're not subject to the law of God and cannot be. They are by nature enemies of God and His laws.

Let's read Romans 8:7–9.

ROMANS 8:7–9

7   *Because* THE CARNAL MIND IS ENMITY
     AGAINST GOD: FOR IT IS NOT SUBJECT TO
     THE LAW OF GOD, NEITHER INDEED CAN BE.

8   *So then they that are in the flesh cannot please*
     God.

9   *But ye are not in the flesh, but in the Spirit, if so*
     be that the Spirit of God dwell in you. Now if any
     man have not the Spirit of Christ, he is none of his.

The unsaved world is not subject to the law of God,
"neither indeed can be" (v. 7). They are by nature enemies
of God. And if they're enemies of God, they're enemies to
the laws of God. James 2:10 says, *"For whosoever shall keep the*
whole law, and yet offend in one point, he is guilty of all."

Let's look at Ephesians 2:11.

EPHESIANS 2:11

11   *Wherefore remember, that ye being in time past*
      Gentiles in the flesh, who are called Uncircumcision
      by that which is called the Circumcision in the flesh
      made by hands.

Paul is writing to the Church at Ephesus, which is, of
course, a Gentile church. But notice that he doesn't call
them Gentiles anymore.

EPHESIANS 2:12

12   *That at that time* [when you were Gentiles in the
      flesh] *ye were without Christ, being aliens from the*
      commonwealth of Israel, and strangers from the
      covenants of promise, having no hope, and without
      God in the world. . . .

Well, what about the statement, "What God has joined
together let no man put asunder" (Matt. 19:6)? God only
joins His own people, not those in the world. Now I don't
know about you, but here's one thing that I would not do as
a minister. I would not marry a Christian to a non-Christian.

God will not join a child of His to a child of the devil. He simply will not do that.

If you join a Christian, a child of God, to a child of the devil, you're going to have problems. If a Christian marries a child of the devil, the Christian is going to have trouble with his father-in-law—the devil. He or she is getting over on his territory.

Church Members

What about modern church members? What marriage law do they abide by? God does not deal with church members. He deals with His own sons and daughters. Just being a church member doesn't make a person a child of God. I was a church member for several years before I became a child of God. Church members may or may not be sons and daughters of God.

The Church's Law—
The Law of Love

I struggled with the subject of marriage, divorce, and remarriage from 1937 to 1949, a twelve-year period. And, as I said, every time I would encounter a different incident concerning this subject, I would start studying again. When I couldn't find the answer, I would give up on it.

In the winter of 1949, I was sitting at my desk studying the subject of marriage, divorce, and remarriage when the Lord spoke to me. I was reading First Corinthians chapter 7 where Paul answered the Church of Corinth's questions concerning marriage and relationships.

I asked myself the question, "What law of marriage, divorce, and remarriage does the Church have?"

And on the inside of me, the Spirit of God said, "The Church doesn't have any!" That boggled my mind.

Without thinking, I almost blurted out, "Why don't we?"

On the inside of me the Spirit of God said, "If the New Testament Church had a law of marriage, divorce, and remarriage, Paul would have given it in First Corinthians, but he didn't, did he?"

So the Church doesn't have a law. Then I asked myself and the Lord this question, "Why doesn't the Church have a law of marriage, divorce, and remarriage?"

And on the inside of me, the answer came back: "Because the Church only has one law—the law of love." The law of love should not only govern marriage, but also the whole life of the believer. Romans 13:10 says, *"Love worketh no ill to his neighbour: therefore love is the fulfilling of the law."*

The minute that hit my spirit, without reading another word from First Corinthians chapter 7, I saw the whole thing from one end of the chapter to the other. It just sprang alive. I received the answer!

I saw what Paul did. He took up different cases that could exist and interpreted them in the light of the law of love. The whole thing became just as clear as a bell to me.

You see, the Corinthians had written Paul and asked him some specific questions about singleness, marriage, divorce, and remarriage. Paul says in First Corinthians 7:1, *"Now concerning the things whereof ye wrote unto me: It is good for a man not to touch a woman."* Paul did not attempt to answer every question that could ever be raised about these subjects. He was simply answering their specific questions in the light of their own culture and circumstances.

There were certain issues they faced back then that we don't face today. Likewise, we may face certain issues today that they didn't have to deal with back then. Paul answered each of their questions by applying the law of love. In other words, he responded by determining the answer to the question, "What would love do?"

Jesus gave this law of love that was to govern the Body of Christ in the last few chapters of the Gospel of John. Jesus is speaking to the disciples just before He went to Calvary— just before he died for our sins and rose from the dead. You see, a new day was dawning, and a New Covenant was coming into existence. Let's look at John 13:34 and 35.

> *JOHN 13:34–35*
>
> 34 *A NEW COMMANDMENT I GIVE UNTO YOU, THAT YE LOVE ONE ANOTHER; as I have loved you, that ye also love one another.*
>
> 35 *By this shall all men know that ye are my disciples, if ye have love one to another.*

God gave us believers a new law. Jesus said, "A new commandment I give you, that ye love one another" (John 13:34). How do we love one another? With natural, human love? Oh, no. That natural, human love can turn to hatred overnight. We love one another with the same kind of love that Christ loved us with—the God-kind of love.

Married Christians

We can love one another as Jesus loved us because the love of Christ has been shed abroad in our hearts (Rom. 5:5). By this shall all men know that we're His disciples, because we have love for one another (John 13:35). Let's read First Corinthians chapter 7 in light of the new commandment.

> *1 CORINTHIANS 7:2–3*
>
> 2 *Nevertheless, to avoid fornication let every man have his own wife, and let every woman have her own husband.*
>
> 3 *Let the husband render unto the wife due benevolence: and likewise also the wife unto the husband.*

God does not want fornication—sexual immorality or impurity in any shape, form, or fashion—to be named among His people (Eph. 5:3). So what does divine love do?

Divine love gives. The intended meaning of First Corinthians 7:3 is, "Withhold not sexual intercourse from one another."

So Paul interprets everything that should happen in the marriage relationship in light of the law of love. Why does the Bible say not to withhold sexual intercourse from one another? Let's look at the next verse.

1 CORINTHIANS 7:4

4   *The wife hath not power of her own body* [authority over her own body], *but the husband* [has authority over her body]: *and likewise also the husband hath not power of his own body, but the wife* [has authority over her husband's body].

Your body doesn't just belong to you. If you're a Christian and are married, it belongs to your spouse also. The husband's body doesn't just belong to him; it also belongs to his wife. And the wife's body doesn't just belong to her; it also belongs to her husband. Paul is interpreting this scripture in light of the law of love. What would divine love do?

1 CORINTHIANS 7:5

5   *Defraud ye not one the other* [withhold not sexual intercourse one from another], *except it be with consent* [that is, both of you consenting to it] *for a time, that ye may give yourselves to fasting and prayer* [if both of you consent]. . . .

Notice that Paul is speaking to husbands and wives who are Christians. He says not to withhold sexual intercourse from one another unless both consent to it, in order to fast and pray.

1 CORINTHIANS 7:5

5   . . . *and come together again* [have sexual intercourse again], *that Satan tempt you not for your incontinency.*

But once the time of fasting and prayer is over, the husband and wife should come together again, because there's great temptation in this area, particularly.

1 CORINTHIANS 7:6

6   *But I speak this by permission, and not of commandment.*

In other words, God didn't command Paul to say this. He was permitted by the Holy Spirit to say it because he was properly interpreting these scriptures in light of the law of love. Remember, verse 2 says, *"Nevertheless, to avoid fornication, let every man have his own wife, and let every woman have her own husband."* God is not commanding that every person be married. Rather, He is saying that those who are married are to meet one another's sexual needs (as well as their own needs). Let's read on.

1 CORINTHIANS 7:7

7   *For I would that all men were even as I myself. But every man hath his proper gift of God, one after this manner, and another after that.*

Paul is not talking about gifts or talents, such as being musically inclined or mechanically skilled. He is talking about singleness (celibacy in particular) and marriage. He indicates that either status is a gift from God. Paul says, "Every man has his proper gift," and Jesus says the same thing in Matthew 19:11: *". . . all men cannot receive this saying, save they to whom it is given."*

The Amplified Bible says, "I wish that all men were like I myself am [in this matter of self-control]. But each has his own special gift from God, one of this kind and one of another" (1 Cor. 7:7). Don't take this scripture out of its setting and make it say something it's not saying. In other words, Paul was saying that some are gifted in such a way that they can be unmarried and be perfectly satisfied.

Unmarried Christians

Then Paul speaks to those who are unmarried. He says that it is better to marry than to be aflame with passion. He interprets the situation in light of the law of love.

1 CORINTHIANS 7:8–9

8 *I say therefore to the unmarried and widows, It is good for them if they abide even as I.*

9 *But IF THEY CANNOT CONTAIN, LET THEM MARRY: for it is better to marry than to burn.*

I remember holding a meeting for a leading Bible scholar, a man who knew more about the Bible than most of the rest of us. He was the pastor of the church where the meeting was being held. We started talking about the subject of marriage, divorce, and remarriage. He had done quite a bit of research and study on this subject.

So this pastor said to me, "We had a young man and a young lady here in the church who were both saved and filled with the Holy Ghost. I performed their wedding ceremony. There was no doubt that God joined them together, as far as that's concerned.

"But in the process of time," he continued, "after two or three years of marriage, she left him, divorced him, and took up with another man. She ran off with the other man, and we never heard from her again. I don't know where she is today."

Some people believe that if God joins two people together in marriage, then they're *always* one, no matter what. Let's look at what Paul says in First Corinthians chapter 6.

1 CORINTHIANS 6:15–16

15 *Know ye not that your bodies are the members of Christ? shall I then take the members of Christ, and make them the members of an harlot? God forbid.*

16 What? know ye not that he which is joined to an harlot [prostitute] **is one body? for two, saith he, shall be one flesh.**

If Paul says that two people become one flesh, how did this husband and wife ever get separated?

The next verse says, *"But he that is joined to the Lord is one spirit"* (1 Cor. 6:17). If you're born again, you're one spirit with the Lord. Can you be separated? Can you be lost? Yes!

If you believe that two people God joined together are forever one flesh and can never be separated, then you would also have to believe in unconditional eternal security. You would have to believe that no matter how a person may backslide, no matter how a person may curse God or renounce Jesus, he would still be eternally joined to the Lord, never to be separated.

Now the young man whose wife left him went right on serving the Lord. He continued working in the church.

"About three or four in the morning," the pastor said, "there was a pounding on the parsonage door. I got out of bed and went to open the door. This young fellow fell onto my living room floor, just bawling and squalling. He had fallen [succumb to sexual immorality]."

"It's better to marry than to be aflame with passion," Paul said in First Corinthians 7:9. He is speaking to the unmarried Christians. The young man who had fallen was not married. Now he had been married, but he had been through a divorce and was not married at the time.

Well, the pastor prayed with him and got him restored. The young man went along for many months, and the same thing happened again. So the pastor said, "I prayed and got him restored to God again." The Bible says that if any person be overtaken in a fault, those who are spiritual should restore the person overtaken in a fault in the spirit of meekness (Gal. 6:1).

Then the pastor sat him down and talked to him: "Young man, I know this is not what you've been taught growing up, and even when I first came here to pastor, it was not what I taught. But I see the Scriptures in a different light. Now you're just a young man. There are many wonderful, beautiful, consecrated young ladies in our church. Find one and get married!"

Remember that we interpret these situations in light of the law of love. What would love do? We've been so legalistic that we've missed divine love. So the young man found someone in the church and remarried. *I say therefore to the unmarried and widows, It is good for them if they abide even as I. But if they cannot contain, let them marry: for it is better to marry than to burn* (1 Cor. 7:8–9).

I was holding a meeting in 1954 in east Texas. The pastor was a young man, about twenty-five years old. He said to me, "Brother Hagin, I have a man in my church who's a retired colonel. He spent thirty-five years in the service and then retired. He is now fifty-seven years old and the only child of a very wealthy family. His mother and father live here and they're in their mid-eighties. He came back here to take care of them.

"After he got into the service, he met a woman and married. They were married for a few years, and then his wife left him for another man. All of his life, he belonged to a denominational church, but he had never been born again.

"When he came back here to take care of his mother and father, someone witnessed to him. He came to the Pentecostal church and received Jesus as his Savior. Then he started seeking to be filled with the Holy Ghost. There were different revivals going on at the time, so he went to church every night. He met a lady at one church he went to. They became interested in each other, and, eventually, he asked her to marry him.

"They went to her pastor to get married, and her pastor asked the colonel, 'Have you ever been married?' Since he had been married and divorced, this pastor said that they couldn't marry. He quoted them the scripture, ' . . . *for two, saith he, shall be one flesh*' (1 Cor. 6:16). He said that this colonel had already become one flesh with his first wife, and if he married another, he would be sinning."

However, the colonel's pastor said to me, "He came to me, and I told him I thought it would be all right. What do you think about it?"

I said, "Sure, it's all right for him to marry."

"The colonel told me that he loves this lady. She's a beautiful Christian. He said that he's not marrying because he needs a woman. He's lived right as a church member and hasn't touched a woman in twenty-five years. He wasn't marrying in order to have sex; he was marrying for companionship." The colonel's pastor continued, "But he didn't want her to go to hell. He said that he wouldn't get married if it would cause her to go to hell. Once I said it was all right, her pastor came to me; he was so angry. He chewed me up and spit me out!"

Then the colonel's pastor asked me if I would talk to her pastor to try and straighten things out. I said that I would. We spent two hours discussing this issue. And every time he would bring up a scripture, I would show him where he was wrong. He would get mad and blow up!

I said, "Now wait a minute. We're brothers. If you can't be a Christian, at least be a gentleman." And he simmered down.

He said, "You're right, Brother Hagin. Forgive me. I got mad because I was getting whipped with the scriptures. You've used the Bible to knock every prop out from under every argument I had. I've got one more scripture, and if you

37

knock the prop out from under me on this one, I'm going to insist that they get married."

I said, "All right, what is it?"

He said, "God joined he and his **first** wife together. If they became one flesh, then how could they ever be separated?" He was referring to First Corinthians 6:16.

I said, "I'm sure glad you asked that question. Open your Bible to First Corinthians chapter 6."

1 CORINTHIANS 6:15–16

15 *Know ye not that your bodies are the members of Christ? shall I then take the members of Christ, and make them the members of an harlot? God forbid.*

16 *What? know ye not that he which is joined to an harlot is one body? for two, saith he, shall be one flesh.*

Then I said to him, "Paul said that a person can be one flesh with a harlot. Remember how you used to tell us about the days before you were saved? You would laugh and tell us how many different women you had. How did you ever separate from each one? According to this scripture, you became one flesh with every one of them. First Corinthians 6:17 says, *'But he that is joined unto the Lord is one spirit.'* If you believe that once you're joined to a person, you can never be separated, then you would also have to believe in eternal security, because he that is joined to the Lord is one spirit. How could you ever be separated from Him, no matter what you did, or decided, if you're one spirit?"

I knew he didn't believe in unconditional eternal security. In other words, a marriage can be dissolved and the two are no longer one flesh, just like a person's relationship with the Lord can be dissolved and they are no longer spiritually united. When the pastor understood what these scriptures meant, he said, "My God, you've knocked every prop out from under every one of my arguments. I'm going to insist that they get married." And they did.

In John chapter 4, Jesus told the woman at the well to go and get her husband. She said to Jesus, "I don't have a husband."

Jesus responded, "You're right; you don't have a husband. But you have had five husbands."

If Jesus believed that a person could never be separated from a spouse, He would have said, "You currently have five husbands." Or, if He believed that a person is always joined to the first person he or she marries, He would have said, "You have only one husband, but your other four marriages were fraudulent." Jesus recognized each of her five marriages. You see, God acknowledges divorce whether He is pleased with it or not.

Divine Love in a Marriage Relationship

Paul wrote First Corinthians to the Church at Corinth. He was telling them to remember the law of love. In a situation where both husband and wife are Christians, the wife should not depart from the husband, nor should the husband put away his wife.

1 CORINTHIANS 7:10–11

10   *And unto the married I command, yet not I, but the Lord, Let not the wife depart from her husband:*

11   *But and if she depart, let her remain unmarried, or be reconciled to her husband: and let not the husband put away his wife.*

Let's interpret this as Paul did, in light of the law of love. Two Christians who are married should abide by the law of love. What would love do? Would love put away his wife? No. Would love depart from her husband? No, love wouldn't do that. I'm not talking about natural, human love; I'm talking about divine love.

First Corinthians chapter 13 says that love endures long and is kind. It's not selfish. Let's read verses 4 through 8 in *The Amplified Bible*. Then we'll see what love would do.

1 CORINTHIANS 13:4-8 (Amplified)

4 *Love endures long and is patient and kind; love never is envious nor boils over with jealousy, is not boastful or vainglorious, does not display itself haughtily.*

5 *It is not conceited (arrogant and inflated with pride); it is not rude (unmannerly) and does not act unbecomingly. Love (God's love in us) does not insist on its own rights or its own way, for it is not self-seeking; it is not touchy or fretful or resentful; it takes no account of the evil done to it (it pays no attention to a suffered wrong).*

6 *It does not rejoice at injustice and unrighteousness, but rejoices when right and truth prevail.*

7 *Love bears up under anything and everything that comes, is ever ready to believe the best of every person, its hopes are fadeless under all circumstances, and it endures everything (without weakening).*

8 *Love never fails (never fades out or becomes obsolete or comes to an end). . . .*

Love would not depart from her husband. That's what love would do. Divine love would not put away his wife.

Love suffers long and is kind. Many times people suffer long, but they're not kind while they're suffering. They just do it because they have to. Love also does not seek its own. Can you see how love will cure the ills in the home? If both husband and wife are walking in the new commandment of divine love, then their marriage will not fail! Now scolding and quarreling have caused marriages to fail. But this Jesus-kind of love never fails!

There has never been an authentic case of two Christians who consistently walked in love ever going to divorce court.

Now I did not say that there has never been a case where two Christians were divorced. I said, "two Christians *who consistently walked in love.*"

According to First Corinthians 13:8, love never fails. If two Christians are walking in love, then their marriage will not fail. If both husband and wife are walking in divine love, neither will even want a divorce. The atmosphere in their home will be so positive. They won't want to get out of that kind of marriage.

If you are having trouble in your marriage and both of you are Christians, you need to write down First Corinthians 13:4–8 from *The Amplified Bible* on a piece of paper. Then both of you need to read it every morning before you get up and every evening before you go to bed. If you will read these verses together and act on the Word, it won't be long until your home will be Heaven on earth. And you can do it, because you have the God-kind of love shed abroad in your hearts (Rom. 5:5).

I remember a splendid Christian man I knew quite well. His wife had been saved, but never filled with the Spirit. Even though she was saved, she didn't walk very close with God. She wasn't very consecrated. That's dangerous. You see, if you're not dedicated to God and separated from the world, you're sort of like the little boy who fell out of bed. His mother heard the thud when he hit the floor and rushed into his room, "What's the matter?"

The little boy said, "Well, I fell out of bed."

She said, "How did you fall out of bed?"

"Well," he said, "I stayed too close to where I got in." He was too close to the edge of the bed. Some folks get saved and then stay too close to where they got in. They eventually fall out of the things of God.

Well, the wife of the Christian man that I knew did just that. She fell out of the things of God and took up with another man whom she lived with for several years. Now she was not divorced from her husband. They hadn't gotten a divorce yet. She was just cohabiting with this other man for about seven years.

Evidently, she didn't want anything to do with her husband. And he had every right in the world to divorce her and remarry if he wanted to. He even began to think about it.

But then she contacted him and wanted to get back to God. She realized that she was a weak person and that without him, she would die and go to hell. She realized that she needed him.

Well, in regard to natural, human love, he didn't have any for her. She just about killed every bit of love that he ever had for her. Natural love is that way, but divine love never fails. It lives forever.

And so he told her, "From the standpoint of the love of God and from the standpoint of saving your soul and from the standpoint of keeping you from going to hell, I'll take you back." So he took her back, even though he didn't have any affection for her whatsoever.

He acted on the love of God that was in him. That's a mighty hard thing to do—to take someone back after they've wronged you in so many ways. There aren't too many people who can do that. There aren't too many people who respond in divine love like that.

In the process of time, I was invited into their home, and on a certain occasion, they prepared a meal. I remember that I saw them holding hands. They were older folks, and once in a while, they would slip around behind one another to get a little hug and a kiss. And I could see that when she looked at him, she just adored him. I could see in her eyes such endearment. She respected him so much. I saw a closeness between them. Even the natural love was restored. So she was saved and kept from going to hell, and besides that, their marriage was totally restored.

We have to ask ourselves the question: "What would divine love do?"

An Unsaved Spouse

Now Paul takes up the case of a marriage relationship where one is a Christian and one is not a Christian.

1 CORINTHIANS 7:12–13

> *12 But to the rest speak I, not the Lord: If any brother hath a wife that believeth not, and SHE BE PLEASED TO DWELL WITH HIM, let him not put her away.*
>
> *13 And the woman which hath an husband that believeth not, and if HE BE PLEASED TO DWELL WITH HER, let her not leave him.*

If an unbelieving wife is running around with other men, then she's not pleased to dwell with her Christian husband. And if an unbelieving husband is running around with other women, then he's not pleased to dwell with his Christian wife. If an unbelieving husband is beating and abusing his believing wife, then he's not pleased to dwell with her. Notice the next verse.

1 CORINTHIANS 7:15

> *15 But if the unbelieving depart* [whether it's the wife or the husband], *let him depart* [or her depart]. *A brother or a sister is not under bondage in such cases: but God hath called us to peace.*

If an unbelieving husband is not pleased to dwell with a Christian wife, the Christian wife is not under bondage to the marriage vows. She can marry again—in the Lord, of course. She can marry another believer. Or if an unbelieving wife is not pleased to dwell with a Christian husband, the Christian husband is not under bondage to the marriage vows. He can marry again.

There was a woman in our church whose husband was unsaved and had a mental problem. She told me once, "One night I woke up, and he was right over me with a butcher knife. I'm scared, Brother Hagin. What am I going to do?"

Well, I had spoken with him when his mind was right. He wasn't against God, Christ, or the Church. He believed that the Bible is true, and he mentally believed that Jesus is the Son of God. But he was not ready to make a commitment. He would tell me to pray for him and not to give up on him. But when I would talk with him, he just wasn't interested. He didn't want to personally accept Jesus as his Savior.

Then something happened, and his mind became worse. You see, he had the opportunity over a period of years to give his heart to God. But he said, "No." And his poor, dear wife was left with so much responsibility, because he was not able to work and she had to take care of the kids. They were surviving on what they could get and what the church could do for them. She almost lost her mind. She became so burdened and so worried that she didn't know what she was doing.

We had to help her. Her husband had been in the service during World War I, so we put him into a veteran's hospital. He just went from bad to worse. Finally, he died there. We took up an offering to help her, and people brought in groceries, and blessed her.

I feel sorry for a lot of these women who choose to stay in a situation like that. They're determined that they're going to get their husband saved, no matter what. But notice that he didn't get saved. If you could always get your spouse saved, then Paul would have said so in First Corinthians. He was writing under the inspiration of the Spirit of God.

1 CORINTHIANS 7:16

16 *For what knowest thou, O wife, whether thou shalt save thy husband? or how knowest thou, O man, whether thou shalt save thy wife?*

In other words, you *might* get your husband saved. If he is pleased to dwell with you and to take his responsibility and place, just stay with him, because you *might* get him saved. Or if your unbelieving wife is pleased to dwell with you, you *might* get her saved. Paul did not say that if you will just believe God, you will always get them saved. God will not override a person's will and make them get saved whether they want to or not. He won't do it!

Many dear women suffer through some things because they think they ought to stay with their husbands. They think they are going to get their husbands saved.

A Christian Spouse Departs

I remember another minister of the Gospel whom I admired greatly. He was a leader of a Full Gospel denomination, a man who had been in an official position. I was preaching in his church. And he asked, "Brother Hagin, what does the Bible mean when it says, 'a believer is not under bondage in such cases'?"

I said, "Well, the way I understand it is that a person in such a situation is not under bondage to the marriage vows."

He said, "That's exactly what I understand it to mean also. No one in the entire world has been any harder than I have about marriage. You see, I came up under the old-line, holiness Pentecostals. And I just accepted what they said. I was as hard as nails about the subject."

This minister lived in quite a large parsonage. His deceased wife's mother and his daughter, who was divorced and had a young boy, lived in the parsonage with him.

"My daughter," he said, "is twenty-eight years old. She's a beautiful girl. Her mother was exceptionally beautiful. I don't mean just pretty; I mean beautiful. And the girl is the same—an exceptionally beautiful girl.

45

"Well," he said, "she grew up in our church. She was saved and filled with the Spirit. Soon she met a young man whose family also grew up in our church. He was from a splendid family background. The young man was also saved, filled with the Spirit, and had been in church all his life. They fell in love. After they graduated from high school, my daughter received some business education and started working. He started working too. Actually, his family owned some businesses, and he began operating one of them. And so, they married.

"Everyone said that it was a perfect match. She became pregnant. Well, he didn't want to have any children. They didn't understand about birth control like we do today. And so, she had a baby boy. And afterwards, her husband came by to see the baby boy, kissed his wife, and said goodbye. We never saw him again. He just left. He disappeared.

"We learned two or three years later that he began practicing homosexuality and was living in that lifestyle. Now here I am, having preached all my life against divorce and remarriage.

"My daughter works; she makes good money. She's a very intelligent woman. I tried to be a daddy to her boy, but I'm an older man. That boy needs someone who can take him fishing and so forth. Pastoring a church takes up all my time. He needs someone who can romp and play with him.

"Seeing my daughter sit in her room and cry night after night finally got to me. One night I threw her door open and said, 'Get out of here and go find a boyfriend!'"

"Why," she said, "Daddy, you preach against divorce and remarriage!"

"I don't care what I preach! It's not the will of God for you to sit here and dry up as an innocent victim! Go get someone! Go circulate with the young folks," he responded.

"Well," she said, "if I start dating someone, then I might fall in love and eventually get married."

"I know it," he said. "Just go ahead and do it."

"She did just what I suggested and now she is dating a splendid man. Her son likes him also. This man had the same kind of experience that my daughter had. While he was away in the service, his wife left him for another fellow. He never heard from her again. So now, my daughter and this man want to get married."

This minister asked me what I thought about their getting married. I said, "I think it's fine."

He said, "I do too. I've been studying the subject. But there's something I don't understand. First Corinthians 7:15 says, *'But if the unbelieving depart, let him depart. A brother or a sister is not under bondage in such cases. . . .'* Paul said that the believer is not under bondage to the marriage vows if his or her unbelieving spouse departs. But in my daughter's situation, her husband was a believer."

I then referred him to First Timothy 5:8, where Paul writing to Timothy said, *"But if any provide not for his own, and specially for those of his own house, he hath denied the faith, and is worse than an infidel."* He is saying that those believers who leave and do not care for their household are worse than infidels. They're worse than unbelievers, because they know better. They've been enlightened. They can't get by as easily as a sinner can, because a sinner doesn't know any better. It's a sinner's nature to act like that.

Along these same lines, consider what Jesus said in Matthew chapter 18.

MATTHEW 18:15–17

15 *Moreover if thy brother shall trespass against thee, go and tell him his fault between thee and him alone: if he shall hear thee, thou hast gained thy brother.*

16 *But if he will not hear thee, then take with thee one or two more, that in the mouth of two or three witnesses every word may be established.*

17 *And if he shall neglect to hear them, tell it unto the church: but if he neglect to hear the church, let him be unto thee as an heathen man and a publican.*

There may be a man who claims to be a Christian but is treating his wife badly, perhaps abusing her severely. The wife may have pleaded with her husband not to treat her that way. Other Christians, including the pastor (who represents the church), may have also talked with the husband. Should the wife stay in a marriage where a so-called "Christian husband" is putting her emotional and physical well-being at risk? Jesus said in Matthew 18:17 that if the offending person continually disregards counsel, he is just like a heathen man. In other words, his conduct is like that of an unbeliever. He is worse than an infidel.

Identify With Christ

Have you ever heard someone say, "I'm trying to find out who I am"? Some people leave their husband or wife in order to find out who they are. They are trying to establish their own identity. That's nothing in the world but human ego and devilish pride. We don't have to establish our own identity. Those of us who are born again are identified with Christ.

If you look back in history, Corinth was one of the most licentious and immoral cities of the east. And that immorality got into the Church. First Corinthians 5 says, *"It is reported commonly that there is fornication among you, and such fornication as is not so much as named among the Gentiles, that one should have his father's wife"* (v.1). In other words, a son had taken his stepmother away from his daddy and was living with her. He was cohabiting with her in open sin. Because Corinth was one of the most immoral cities, that same immoral spirit got into the Church.

I remember a RHEMA graduate who would occasionally go on long fasts. Every time he did, he would come up with some kooky idea. One time he went on a fast for 18 days, and he said that the Lord told him to send his wife back to her parents. Well, the Lord would never do that. God is not tearing up homes.

So his wife said to him, "What's the matter? What's wrong?"

He responded, "Well, we have different goals in life."

She said, "No, I don't have any other goals except to just back you up in the ministry. I'll go wherever you want to go. That's my only goal."

"Well, no," he said. "I'm going to send you back to your parents. God told me to."

She said, "Tell me what's the matter. What can I do? I'll change. I love you. I believe God put us together. I'm willing to change. You just tell me."

In response, he said, "No! There's nothing wrong with you. We just have different goals in life."

Matthew 19:3 says, ". . . *Is it lawful for a man to put away his wife for every cause?*" Is "different goals" a Bible cause to put his wife away? No! One of the main problems here is that he was not walking in the light of the Word. If he would have only listened to what the Bible says, it would have solved a lot of his problems. No matter how much you fast, if you're not going to walk in the light of the Word, you will be walking in darkness.

Let's go back to the beginning. In Genesis chapter 2, we see just how God thinks about marriage.

GENESIS 2:22–24

22 *And the rib, which the Lord God had taken from man, made he a woman, and brought her unto the man.*

23 *And Adam said, This is now bone of my bones, and flesh of my flesh: she shall be called Woman, because she was taken out of Man.*

49

> 24 *Therefore shall a man leave his father and his mother, and shall cleave unto his wife: and they shall be one flesh.*

I think many people want to take the "c" out of "cleave" and make it "leave" his wife. But the scripture says that a husband is to leave his father and mother, not his wife.

If you want to be in full fellowship with God, you're going to have to walk in the light His Word. If you don't walk in the light of the Bible, you're in so much darkness. The entrance of His Word gives light (Ps. 119:130). The Bible says that a husband is to leave his father and mother and cleave unto his wife (Gen. 2:24).

Stay Where You Are

Each case must stand on its own merits. You can't just lay down iron-clad rules that are going to regulate every case. You have to learn to interpret whatever is happening by the law of love. Let's continue in First Corinthians.

> *1 CORINTHIANS 7:16–20*
>
> 16 *For what knowest thou, O wife, whether thou shalt save thy husband? or how knowest thou, O man, whether thou shalt save thy wife?*
>
> 17 *But as God hath distributed to every man, as the Lord hath called every one, so let him walk. And so ordain I in all churches.*
>
> 18 *Is any man called being circumcised? let him not become uncircumcised. Is any called in uncircumcision? let him not be circumcised.*
>
> 19 *Circumcision is nothing, and uncircumcision is nothing, but the keeping of the commandments of God.*
>
> 20 *LET EVERY MAN ABIDE in the same calling wherein he was called.*

Now we must interpret this within the context of what Paul is discussing. If you've been married forty times and

you and your current wife just got saved, stay right where
you are.

Some people believe that you have to go back to the
original person you married because you became one flesh
with them. How could you go back to him or her, anyway?
No, you abide right where you are.

1 CORINTHIANS 7:21-24

21 *Art thou called being a servant? care not for it: but
if thou mayest be made free, use it rather.*

22 *For he that is called in the Lord, being a servant, is
the Lord's freeman: likewise also he that is called,
being free, is Christ's servant.*

23 *Ye are bought with a price; be not ye the servants
of men.*

24 *Brethren, LET EVERY MAN, WHEREIN HE IS
CALLED, THEREIN ABIDE WITH GOD.*

Now, you see, Paul is still on the same subject. He's
interpreting the situation in light of the law of love. If you
get saved after you are already married, you simply go on
living for God. You abide in that husband-and-wife relationship. Let's continue to read.

1 CORINTHIANS 7:25-26

25 *Now concerning virgins I have no commandment of
the Lord: yet I give my judgment, as one that hath
obtained mercy of the Lord to be faithful.*

26 *I suppose therefore that this is good for the present
distress, I say, that it is good for a man so to be.*

Notice that Paul is still on the same subject. Don't take
these verses out of context, but instead realize that Paul is
using each of these points to illustrate something about the
subject of marriage. Paul is giving his advice by the Spirit of
God to a man or woman who is a virgin, one that has not
been married before. He says that in light of the law of love
and of the circumstances (the present distress) under which

they lived at that time, it was good for a man or woman to remain a virgin.

1 CORINTHIANS 7:27–28

27 *Art thou bound unto a wife? seek not to be loosed. Art thou loosed from a wife? seek not a wife.*

28 *But and if thou marry, thou hast not sinned; and if a virgin marry, she hath not sinned. Nevertheless such shall have trouble in the flesh: but I spare you.*

If a man is already married, he should stay married to his wife. But, as Paul says, "If a husband has been loosed from a wife, he should not seek a wife" (1 Cor. 7:27). To be loosed from a wife speaks of divorce. It can mean an unbelieving wife left or a Christian woman backslid and went off with some other fellow. But if the man who has been "loosed from a wife" chooses to remarry, he has not sinned (see 1 Cor. 7:28).

Now in verse 28, Paul goes back to talking to virgins (those who had never been married). He interprets these conditions in light of the law of love. If a virgin marries, he or she has not sinned.

Then Paul says, *". . . Nevertheless such shall have trouble in the flesh: but I spare you"* (1 Cor. 7:28). What does it mean to "have trouble in the flesh"? First Corinthians 7:28 in *The Amplified Bible* says, ". . . Yet those who marry will have physical and earthly troubles, and I would like to spare you that."

Let's continue reading.

1 CORINTHIANS 7:29–35

29 *But this I say, brethren, the time is short: it remaineth, that both they that have wives be as though they had none;*

30 *And they that weep, as though they wept not; and they that rejoice, as though they rejoiced not; and they that buy, as though they possessed not;*

31 *And they that use this world, as not abusing it: for the fashion of this world passeth away.*

32 *But I would have you without carefulness. He that is unmarried careth for the things that belong to the Lord, how he may please the Lord:*

33 *But he that is married careth for the things that are of the world, how he may please his wife.*

34 *There is difference also between a wife and a virgin. The unmarried woman careth for the things of the Lord, that she may be holy in body and in spirit: but she that is married careth for the things of the world, how she may please her husband.*

35 *But this I speak for your own profit; not that I may cast a snare upon you, but for that which is comely, and that ye may attend upon the Lord without distraction.*

Paul is still saying that it's not a sin to marry. He is not trying to put them under bondage. Jesus said the same thing in Matthew 19:12: "There are eunuchs that are born that way. There are eunuchs that have been made that way by men. And there are eunuchs that have been made that way for the Kingdom of Heaven's sake. But everyone can't accept this saying. It's only given to them that can accept it."

Do you see how clear it all becomes when you interpret the Scripture in light of the law of love? No matter what the past has been, you can forget about it and go on with God. You can abide where you are called.

God has given us His ideal of marriage in His Word. So what we need to do is to take the time and effort to excel in God's ideal of marriage. We can start right where we are.

If you've been married forty times, forget about it. That's all in the past. Abide where you are. Work on God's ideal of marriage. If you've never been married, find out what the Scripture says before you get married, and you'll know how to work on it and make it successful from the beginning.

The Past Is in the Past

In a church that I once pastored, our pianist had a sixteen-year-old daughter who could also play the piano. Now the daughter wasn't as accomplished as the mother. The mother would play on Sunday mornings, and the daughter would play on Wednesday evenings. The mother began to have some physical problems. Her local doctor sent her away to a larger city for treatment, and they discovered that she had a tumor in her lung as large as a person's fist.

Back in 1939 this was very serious. The kind of operation she needed was risky. Doctors have learned so much since then, but at that time, the percentage of survival was small for the condition she had. So they decided to give her X-ray treatments. The treatments were supposed to shrivel that tumor. And if it didn't diminish, then the next step was an operation. She traveled to this larger city twice a week for these treatments.

She never asked for prayer. She never asked me to anoint her with oil or lay hands on her. Her daughter would come to church to play the piano when her mother couldn't make it and say, "Pray for Momma; she's not feeling well." So we all prayed for her mother in a general way. Or sometimes her husband would come to church and say, "Pray for my wife." And we would pray for her. But she never came for special prayer.

One Sunday morning I had just finished my message and the word of the Lord came to me, "There is a woman I want to heal before you go today." So I just spoke out to the congregation that the Lord wanted to heal a woman before we dismissed. You see, when the Lord spoke this to me, we were already standing, and I was about to dismiss everyone.

We had three sections of seats in our auditorium. A woman got up and stepped out into the aisle. She started walking down to the front. And on the inside of me, I knew that she was not the one. I said, "You're not the one, sister, but come on down and I'll lay hands on you anyway. Healing belongs to you."

Then about that time, I saw the woman who played the piano for us step out and come down. On the inside of me, the Spirit of God said, "She's the one."

I said, "You're the one." I laid hands on her.

On Tuesday she went back to the doctor for her X-ray treatment. She said to the doctor, "I want you to take a picture of my lungs." The doctor wanted to know why.

She said, "Something has happened. Go ahead and take the picture. Then I'll tell you."

He didn't want to, but she said, "I'm paying for it. You just go ahead and do it." They took the picture. They had to wait all day for it to be developed. It took longer in those days.

The doctor finally came out and said, "If it's all right, we would like to take another picture. This won't cost you anything. It's on the house." So they took another one. They ended up taking five different pictures of her in five different positions. After they finished taking and developing all five, they called her husband in. They showed him the picture of the one they'd taken with the growth beforehand. All five that they had recently taken showed no growth at all. All five pictures were clear!

They said, "We don't understand it. We never would have believed it if we didn't have this picture to prove it." So the husband told the doctors what had happened.

They said, "Well, one thing about it; it sure worked, didn't it!"

Some time later, she was testifying in church. She said, "Of course, you folks don't know about my past. But I was just sure that God wouldn't heal me. I knew I loved the

Lord, but I've been married and divorced four times. I didn't have enough nerve to come up here for healing."

But God went after her, anyway. When she got born again, God forgot about her past. He didn't have any knowledge of it. It was all gone! And twenty-five years later, I spoke with her, and she was still well!

I had a pastor friend share with me about three young couples he had in his church. All three couples were in their late twenties and early thirties. They all came to his church and got saved. In the process of time, one of the young men felt God calling him to preach. So the pastor tried to help him. He gave him the opportunity to work with the youth and teach some Sunday school classes.

This pastor was not only the pastor of this church, but he also was the presbyter of a particular denomination for the Fort Worth section. There was another little church in the suburbs of Fort Worth that needed a pastor. This was many years ago when Fort Worth was much smaller. The little church only had half a dozen or so members, and about twenty or thirty people showed up for the services. So this pastor sent this young man from his church.

After being there a year, he still had only twenty-five or thirty people coming to the services. So he quit. Before he quit, he applied for a license because he needed to be able to perform weddings and funerals. The licensing organization asked him, "Are you married? Have you ever been divorced?" And neither he nor his wife had ever been divorced, so they gave him the license.

Well, another young couple from this pastor's church also felt called into ministry. So he sent them to pastor that little church in the suburbs of Fort Worth. They stayed about a year and then left. The young man also got licensed. They asked him the same questions they asked the first young man, and he also said, "No, problem. I've never been divorced."

Finally, the third couple felt called into the ministry. So the pastor sent them to this little church. They hadn't been there six months and were already running over 100 people. They started building a new building. So he needed a license to legally marry people. He filled out the questionnaire. He had never been divorced, but his wife had been. She was divorced before she ever got saved. Because of this, they wouldn't give him a license. They wouldn't put their stamp of approval on him. Yet he did more for that church than all the rest of them.

The pastor helped him get licensed with another organization. He stayed at that church and built it up to several hundred. The other two young men who were licensed have been sitting around for thirty years, doing nothing in ministry. But God just blessed this one fellow.

When people come to know the Lord, whatever happened in their past is gone. First Corinthians chapter 7 explains that whatever state a man is in when the grace of God comes to him, he should stay there. If he has been married and divorced three or four times before he got saved and is now married, he should stay right where he is and go on with God. Likewise, if he is single, he shouldn't feel automatically compelled to get married. God meets us right where we are.

CHAPTER FOUR

God's Ideal of Marriage

God's ideal of marriage is described in Ephesians chapter 5. You can begin wherever you are—whether single, married, divorced, or remarried—and go on with God.

EPHESIANS 5:22–33

 22 Wives, submit yourselves unto your own husbands, as unto the Lord.

 23 For the husband is the head of the wife, even as Christ is the head of the church: and he is the saviour of the body.

 24 Therefore as the church is subject unto Christ, so let the wives be to their own husbands in every thing.

 25 HUSBANDS, LOVE YOUR WIVES, EVEN AS CHRIST ALSO LOVED THE CHURCH, and gave himself for it;

 26 That he might sanctify and cleanse it with the washing of water by the word,

27 *That he might present it to himself a glorious church, not having spot, or wrinkle, or any such thing; but that it should be holy and without blemish.*

28 *So ought men to love their wives as their own bodies. He that loveth his wife loveth himself.*

29 *For no man ever yet hated his own flesh; but nourisheth and cherisheth it, even as the Lord the church:*

30 *For we are members of his body, of his flesh, and of his bones.*

31 *For this cause shall a man leave his father and mother, and shall be joined unto his wife, and they two shall be one flesh.*

32 *This is a great mystery: but I speak concerning Christ and the church.*

33 *Nevertheless let every one of you in particular so love his wife even as himself; and the wife see that she reverence her husband.*

Paul tells husbands to love their wives. Well, obviously they have some natural love for one another, or they never would have married to begin with.

But Paul is not talking about natural love here, because he said, *". . . even as Christ also loved the church. . ."* (Eph. 5:25). That's way beyond natural. That far exceeds human love. Christ loved the Church with divine love. It was divine love in operation.

This letter written to the Ephesians could not apply to sinners. An unsaved man could not love his wife as Christ loved the Church. That would be impossible! He doesn't have that kind of love inside him. He has a natural, human love for his wife, but not a divine love.

In the Book of Ephesians, Paul is talking to Christians, where both husband and wife are Christians. Notice that Christian husbands have a potential to love their wives in a way that sinner husbands cannot love their wives, because the love of God—the God-kind of love—has been shed abroad in their hearts by the Holy Ghost.

Now natural, human love can be selfish. And even though the love of God may be in your heart as a Christian, you can still be selfish. If you're walking more in the natural than you are in the spiritual, then your love will be selfish. You will be primarily interested in yourself! But the God-kind of love is unselfish.

God's ideal of marriage is revealed in Ephesians chapter 5. And what you need to do is pick up wherever you are and build your marriage on God's ideal.

A good marriage doesn't just happen. You have to work at it, just like you do anything else. For example, you may be called to ministry, but it doesn't just happen and success is not automatic. You have something to do with it. The same is true with a marriage!

In talking about marriage, we often start reading Ephesians 5:22, where Paul tells wives to submit themselves to their own husbands. But if we go back a few verses, Paul gives instructions to the whole Church at Ephesus.

EPHESIANS 5:18–22

18 *And be not drunk with wine, wherein is excess; but be filled with the Spirit;*

19 *Speaking to yourselves in psalms and hymns and spiritual songs, singing and making melody in your heart to the Lord;*

20 *Giving thanks always for all things unto God and the Father in the name of our Lord Jesus Christ;*

21 *Submitting yourselves one to another in the fear of God.*

22 *Wives, submit yourselves unto your own husbands, as unto the Lord.*

In verse 21, Paul speaks to the Church at Ephesus—telling them to submit themselves to one another. Then in verse 22, he brings up the marriage relationship.

By taking a scripture out of its setting, you can make it say anything you want it to say. Many times people quote verse 22 out of context. They say, "Wives, submit yourselves unto your husbands, as unto the Lord." They leave the impression that the man is the dictator of the home, and the woman is supposed to do whatever the man says to do. Well, if that's the case, we in the Church are supposed to be dictators over one another as well, because verse 21 tells the whole Church at Ephesus to "submit themselves to one another." That would be chaotic.

So what does Paul really mean? When he said, "submitting yourselves to one another" (Eph. 5:21), he meant giving in to one another or getting along with one another. He didn't mean for one person in the Church to be the dictator over everyone else, or for everyone else in the Church to be little dictators. He meant that it is easy to submit to the rule of love.

Paul meant the same thing when he said, "Wives, submit yourselves unto your own husbands," in the very next verse.

You see, by taking a verse out of its setting, you can make a scripture say something that it doesn't actually say.

Error Concerning Submission

Let's continue reading in Ephesians chapter 5.

EPHESIANS 5:23-25

23 *For THE HUSBAND IS THE HEAD OF THE WIFE, even as Christ is the head of the church: and he is the saviour of the body.*

24 *Therefore as the church is subject unto Christ, so let the wives be to their own husbands in every thing.*

25 *Husbands, love your wives, even as Christ also loved the church, and gave himself for it. . . .*

Every twenty-five or thirty years, it seems the same error comes around again. Someone says they have a new revelation. It will last for a little while and then die down. Some get into error by overemphasizing the fact that the husband is the head of the wife. Some people say that the wife doesn't have any say-so whatsoever. They believe that the husband has the right to treat her like a doormat.

I remember my wife and I were having lunch one time with a certain man and his wife. I noticed that the wife didn't say anything. She was just like a little kid who had been continually intimidated. At one time, early on in their marriage, she had been a schoolteacher. But at the time we met with them, she was so bowed down; we could detect that there was something wrong with her.

As my wife and I visited with them, I noticed that the husband did all the talking. My wife picked up on the fact that his wife wasn't saying anything. So she worked the conversation around, and, finally, this man's wife spoke up and said, "Brother Hagin, do you think that a wife has any say-so at all? I mean, can she speak in her own home?"

I said, "Certainly!" I noticed the husband looked "daggers" through me! I saw where the problem was right away. He wanted to dominate and control her. He wanted her to do exactly what he told her to do. She couldn't even speak unless he allowed her to.

At the end of the meal, the husband wanted me to pray for his wife, because she was facing an operation. She was nervous and depressed. I was not surprised. She was living with a fool! A fellow like that is foolish. And really, the main thing that was wrong with her was simply her nerves.

As we checked into this situation, we found out that she couldn't even speak in her own home unless he gave her permission. She couldn't even give her opinion on anything.

This man took a few scriptures out of context. And you can readily see that you could twist these scriptures in Ephesians chapter 5 and make them say that the husband is to dominate the wife, if you wanted to. But that's not what the Scripture is saying, because if you go on and read the next verse, it says, *"Husbands, love your wives, even as Christ also loved the church . . ."* (Eph. 5:25). It definitely wasn't the law of love that this man was demonstrating!

Now on another occasion, I remember a minister whom I invited to come and preach in my church. We really didn't need a meeting, but we were just trying to help him. He got to the point where he didn't have any place to preach. He had two small children, just about the same age as our children. And so, I gave him a meeting to help him. We took up more money for him than anyone else I ever had preach at the church. We also bought him and his wife some clothes while they were there.

We began to discuss this very subject of submission, because I'd been around him before. And I saw how he treated his wife and two little children. He treated his wife badly. She had no say-so. She had to do exactly what he told her to do. He used Ephesians 5:22, *"Wives, submit yourselves unto your own husbands, as unto the Lord."* But he took the scripture out of context. He forgot about the next verse, which reminds husbands to love their wives as Christ loved the Church.

I talked to the poor fellow about his family. I told him that he needed to change the way he treated his wife and two children. I said, "You're going to lose your children. They're going to grow up not knowing a thing in the world about love. They are going to think that God is like you."

He was able to preach well, even though his life wasn't right with God. And we had a good meeting—one of the best meetings we ever had. More people were saved and baptized with the Holy Ghost than in any other meeting.

Later on, he took a church, and I held a meeting for him. I stayed in the parsonage with him and his family. I talked to him again. I remember we discussed Scripture together. And he was the kind of fellow who thought he was always right and everyone else was wrong. If you didn't agree with him, he would put you down.

Well, he didn't know the Word of God as well as I did, so I won every argument. He would quote one scripture, and I would quote two. Finally, he would run out of scriptures, and I would still be quoting them.

Eventually, he said, "Well, I could be wrong. I don't think I am, but I could be."

We were eating at the table discussing these things, when he got a phone call. As a pastor, he needed to visit someone. So after he left, his wife and mother-in-law said, "That's the first time we've ever heard him even insinuate that there's a possibility that he could be wrong."

Well, I saw a momentary change in him, but he went right back to that same dogmatic, dictatorial attitude—always saying that he was right. You could even see it in his preaching. He thought that he was right, and everyone else was wrong.

His two children ended up just as I said they would. I told him exactly what would happen if he continued to treat them badly. I didn't have a revelation. I just knew what the Word of God says. There is a law of sowing and reaping that carries over into every part of a person's life.

We sometimes emphasize sowing and reaping in connection with financial giving. Well, that's true, because Jesus said, *"Give, and it shall be given unto you; good measure, pressed down, and shaken together, and running over, shall men give into your bosom. For with the same measure that ye mete withal it shall be measured to you again"* (Luke 6:38). But, you see, the law of sowing and reaping is true in every other area of life as well.

When his last child graduated from high school, both of them said, "We've had enough of this. Goodbye. We're gone!" And they left. His wife then said, "I've put up with this all these years. The children are grown now. Goodbye. I'm gone."

As far as I know, this man died around the age of forty. He was found dead in bed, alone. He brought it on himself. And to my knowledge, neither one of his children or his wife were serving God when I last heard of them; they hadn't been to church in years. They thought that God was like him. The children grew up with that idea, with that father image. They associated God the Father with their earthly father. But, thank God, He is not like that!

Take Care of Your Wife

Another man I was preaching for one time had a small church. They didn't have any singers in the church. So the husband and wife would sing specials; they were excellent singers. They would usually sing a special every night just before I preached.

I would sit down off the platform and then go up on the platform when I got ready to preach. I wanted to sit out front and listen to them sing. Because it was a smaller building and they didn't have a sound system, I really couldn't hear them very well from behind. Their specials were such a blessing. Well, during the preaching, his wife sat down off the platform because she had two children to watch—one was two-and-a-half years old and the other one was four years old. They didn't have a nursery in such a small church. So he would call her up to the platform to sing.

I noticed that when she would go up to the platform, the whole back of one leg of her hosiery had a huge run in it. I don't see how in the world she ever got those hose on! Every night and every day I was there in the parsonage, I would hear her ask him for money for hose. Back in those days, you could buy a pair of hose for under a dollar.

Her husband would spend money carelessly, never even offering to give her money for a new pair of hose. He was always dressed very nicely. And she didn't have enough clothes to get out of the house with. She couldn't buy anything.

So after three or four nights, he and I were in town one day. I was driving, and I pulled up in front of one of the dry goods stores. I handed him some money and said, "I want you to go buy your wife a pair of hose." He looked at me sort of startled.

I said, "If you don't love her enough as your wife to buy her a pair of hose, I love her enough as a mother to those two young children and as a sister in the Lord. I'm tired of seeing her traipse up to the platform every single night to help you sing with the whole back side out of one leg of her hose!"

This man was certainly not acting in love, wasting his money every day on himself. He could have used that money to buy his wife *several* pairs of hose.

So he said to me, "Oh, no! I have the money. I'll buy her a pair; you just keep that."

I said, "You told her that you didn't have any money."

"Well, I really wasn't paying attention to what she was saying," he said.

"Why don't you ever look at your wife's legs? Besides that, she has told you every day that she needs a new pair of hose. I've heard her ask you."

"I thought she was just going on," he said.

I said, "Go get her a pair, then, if you've got the money, and quit lying about it." So he went into the store and bought her a pair of hose.

Another pastor I was holding a meeting for was exactly the same way. Even though it was during World War II and prices were frozen, he drove a new automobile and wore the finest suits. Well, he had three children. The oldest one was not old enough to go to school yet; a child started school at the age of six back then. The youngest one was just a baby, only two or three months old.

His wife had some serious problems in carrying the last child. They thought she was going to lose it. So when the baby was born, they delivered the child by cesarean section.

Now she was doing all the housework and cooking every meal. I stayed in the parsonage and saw her doing all of this, in addition to taking care of the three kids. She had to get those kids ready for church and then once they got to church, she had to seat them on the pew with her and make sure they were taken care of when she got up to sing with her husband. And the poor dear didn't have any decent clothes. Yet he was dressed nicely from head to toe.

She wasn't very strong. She hadn't recuperated completely yet. And he was fussing at her all the time, saying, "Why don't you do this? Why don't you do that?" Nevertheless, she was so kind and nice to him.

She said to me, "I have three kids to look after, and if the meals are not ready right on time, the way he wants them, he throws a fit! And he quotes the scripture that wives should submit to their husbands."

One day she was outside behind the house washing the laundry over one of those old-fashioned rub boards. That's hard work; I've done it before. And so I said to her, "Isn't there a self-service laundromat here in town?"

She said, "Brother Hagin, there was one, but it burned down."

I said, "Why don't you get someone to wash the clothes for you?"

"There is a lady in the church that has a maid who works for her," she said. "She offered to pay her to do the washing, but my husband said, 'No, we're not going to do that.'"

"You go ahead and tell her to send her maid on over. I will pay for it."

She said, "Oh, no! He wouldn't like that."

I told her I would talk to him. I could tell that she was afraid of him. A wife shouldn't be afraid of her husband, especially if he's a preacher! Obviously, this man was not walking in love.

I am not afraid of Jesus. I love and respect Him. I reverence Him, but I'm not afraid of Him. Why? Because I know that He loves me. The Bible says that husbands should love their wives as Christ loved the Church (Eph. 5:25).

So I said to her husband, "She wouldn't take the money, because I could tell that she's afraid. She almost started trembling. You shouldn't let your wife do all that work; she's not physically able to. She's not even over that operation."

He said, "Well, what's a woman for?" My fleshly nature wanted to slap him. I didn't care if he was a preacher. Even with a fellow like that, you've got to walk in love and put your flesh under.

So I took the money out of my pocket and said to him, "Why don't you go to another town and do the laundry yourself, at one of those self-service laundromats? You have a good car."

"I'm not about to do a woman's work!" A fellow like that is so ignorant; it's a wonder someone doesn't have to come by and tell him to get out of the rain!

Then I mentioned the lady in his church who offered to do the laundry for her. Then I offered him money myself, and he said, "I have money."

So I said, "Listen, if you don't love your wife enough as your wife and the mother of your children to take care of her, I love her enough as a sister in the Lord." He reluctantly agreed to do the laundry. Then, some time later, he took up with another woman. The home was broken, and his ministry ended.

The husband should love the wife, just as Christ loves the Church. The husband should nourish and cherish his wife as Christ cherishes His own Body. The husband cherishes his wife's health and happiness by putting her first. He loves her better than he does himself. And she loves him with God's divine love.

God must have loved us better than He did Himself, because He gave His only begotten Son while we were yet sinners (John 3:16; Rom. 5:8). Others will know that we are disciples of Christ because of the love we have for one another (John 13:35).

Walk in Love

If a wife couldn't do anything unless her husband told her to, then a wife couldn't get saved unless her husband said she could get saved. She couldn't go to Heaven unless her husband said so. She couldn't receive the baptism of the Holy Ghost unless he said so. She couldn't get her prayers answered unless he said so. Yet we know plenty of women who have become great prayer warriors and their husbands either weren't saved or were poor examples of a Christian.

In Smith Wigglesworth's life story, he said that he owed his ministry to his wife. Before he started preaching, he was in business as a plumber. He grew cold and didn't go to church much. He became quite cantankerous. He said to his wife one day, "You're up there at that church all the time. You might as well move your bed up there."

She said, "No, Smith, I'm not up there all the time. I'm up there about three times a week. I do not neglect you, and I do not neglect the children. You know that."

He said, "The Bible says that the man is the head of the house and that wives are to obey their husbands. So I'm telling you not to go to church anymore."

She said, "You are my husband. Whatever you say here in the house goes. But you're not my Lord. Jesus is my Lord, and He said to go, so I'm going to church. Goodbye."

"I'm going to lock you out so you can't get back in!" he said. Evidently, she didn't have a key to the house. So he locked her out.

When she returned, she sat out on the back steps all night. He came downstairs the next morning and unlocked the door. It must have been cool because he found her all huddled up. She was leaning against the door, and when he opened it, she almost fell into the kitchen.

She got up smiling and laughing and said, "Dear, what would you like for breakfast?" She acted as if nothing had happened. She just loved him. Then he felt convicted.

Smith Wigglesworth said that if it hadn't been for his wife (used by God, of course), he would have never made it. He became a great man of God. He was mightily used. And his wife had a big part in all of it. What if his wife had listened to him and quit going to church? They both would have backslid. Who knows where they would have ended up.

I remember when I first started preaching. I pastored a little church out in the country, and I was just a single boy, only 19 years old. As a pastor, I had to deal with problems in the church, even marriage problems.

One man and his wife got into a disagreement. The wife was saved and baptized with the Holy Spirit; she spoke in other tongues. However, the husband was newly saved and had not been baptized with the Holy Spirit. But he was a good man.

Well, I've said it before: Two people can disagree without being disagreeable. Husbands and wives ought to learn to disagree without being disagreeable. Two people don't have to get into a fight; they can disagree respectfully. I've never fought with my wife. We've certainly disagreed, but we have always resolved the situation in love.

Now in this particular situation, the wife was 100 percent wrong! I had dealt with them before, and the wife was usually right. But on this specific occasion, she was wrong. I went to their house, and she was so mad! She didn't even want him in the room where she was. He didn't dare go in. So he stood outside and told me his side of the story.

When I went into their house, she let me know right away that she was right. I just listened. I didn't say anything. She said, "We've been married 15 years, and I want you to know that in 15 years, I've never been wrong!"

I said, "Sister, you're a liar." Well, that so shocked her that she didn't say anything; she just finally shut up!

I continued, "I know better! I know that within 15 years time, you haven't been perfect all the way through. You've made mistakes. And in every kind of disagreement with your husband, you haven't always been 100 percent right. I just know! I'm not very old, but I have enough sense to know that no one is perfect!"

She started to protest again, but I took over and said, "Be quiet and listen to me. I've dealt with situations between you and your husband before, and I'll admit that in the past, you've been right most of the time. Your husband is usually the one who ends up saying, 'Well, she's right, and I'm wrong.'

"But," I said, "in this particular case, you're 100 percent wrong!" She looked at me and began to cry.

She said, "You know, you're exactly right! I guess the first thing I ought to do is repent for saying that I've always been right."

So she called her husband inside and said, "I'm 100 percent wrong. Please forgive me." They got things straightened out, and I don't remember ever having to deal with any situation there again. I'm sure they had some differences, but they got them straightened out. You see, she saw herself. She saw how selfish she had become. She had stopped walking in love.

I remember one fellow came to me crying and weeping. He said that his wife was going to leave him and he didn't know what to do about it. So I asked him, "Why is she going to leave you?"

He said, "I got mad at her and told her I didn't love her anymore. Now I don't know what to do."

I said, "Bless God, repent and go ask her to forgive you. Do what the Bible says to do and straighten up. Do you love her?" He responded that he did love her.

Then I said, "Well, go tell her you love her. And then act like it. Don't just say it; back it up with actions!"

Another fellow came to me, and God told me to help him. My wife and I talked with both he and his wife. Before they were saved, they were all messed up. She had never been married and had two illegitimate children. And he had been married, but his wife left him. But then, they both got saved, were baptized with the Holy Ghost, and met in church. And they were married.

So this fellow came to me and said, "My wife's going to leave me because she's mad at me."

"Why?" I asked.

"Well," he said, "I don't always act in love."

I said, "You ought to."

At the time I didn't know what he was doing, but I found out later he wasn't treating her two children right. He was mean to them; he would call them terrible names. So I said to him, "If you keep treating those children like that, you'll turn them away from God. And you're going to have to love your wife and put her first. Put her before yourself. And act right."

Finally, we got both of them together. I really didn't think that they were going to make it. But they did, thank God. Some time later, my wife and I received a beautiful letter from them; they were out in the ministry, working for God and happy.

I remember seeing them both in one of our seminars. The minister at the pulpit made a call for people to come down to the front to consecrate themselves to be missionaries or to get a worldwide vision. Well, I was sitting on the platform, and I saw this fellow get up out of his seat and walk about 10 feet. Then he stopped and went back and got hold of his wife's arm to escort her down to the front. He treated her as if she were a princess. You see, he began to act right. He began to love her like Jesus loves the Church. And she began to respond to him.

God's Plan for a Companion or Helpmeet

God is love. And man was God's creation. Therefore, man was a creation of love. When God created woman to be man's companion and helpmeet, He took part of man and, out of that, He formed the woman. The woman became flesh of his flesh and bone of his bone (Gen. 2:23).

Now notice in the Book of Ephesians that Paul made reference to what God did in Genesis—how God made woman out of man. *"So ought men to love their wives as their own bodies. He that loveth his wife loveth himself"* (Eph. 5:28).

The Lord also said, *". . . It is not good that the man should be alone; I will make him an help meet for him"* (Gen. 2:18). Actually, the Hebrew word for "helpmeet" means *an answering unto.* I think that's the most unique expression in this wonderful description. Woman was made to answer to the heart need, the spiritual need, the mental need, and the physical need of man.

And when man and woman are married, they are to be a distinct unit, utterly separated from all other humans. Let's read how God formed woman and then made man and woman one flesh.

GENESIS 2:21–24

21 *And the Lord God caused a deep sleep to fall upon Adam, and he slept: and he took one of his ribs, and closed up the flesh instead thereof;*

22 *And the rib, which the Lord God had taken from man, made he a woman, and brought her unto the man.*

23 *And Adam said, This is now bone of my bones, and flesh of my flesh: she shall be called Woman, because she was taken out of Man.*

24 *Therefore shall a man leave his father and his mother, and shall cleave unto his wife: and they shall be one flesh.*

Now this portion of Scripture has within it some of the richest facts about marriage that have ever been written. The man shall leave his mother and father. The wife shall leave her mother and father. And the two shall constitute a home. This is the beginning of the home life, or the family life.

Therefore, God's ideal for marriage is for a man to leave his parents and a woman to leave her parents, and then for the two to become one. When I say, "leave their father and mother," I don't mean that the couple isn't supposed to visit their parents. I mean that the couple's parents are not supposed to be the boss of their home!

There have been more problems created in a home because a mother-in-law or a father-in-law wanted to tell the couple what to do. It's okay to advise people, but it's not okay to run other people's lives—even if they are your children. When they become adults, they are accountable to God themselves.

I remember two RHEMA graduates. The young man was a good, successful minister. They met and decided to get married. At first, her mother said that it was fine. But then her mother got hold of some erroneous teaching and said, "No matter how old you are, you're still supposed to obey your parents. You can marry him, but you have to wait a year."

She was in her mid-twenties. She said, "Well, no, we've already planned everything."

Her mother said, "Now, you are in disobedience."

They both called me long distance, crying on the telephone. The young lady said, "What am I going to do? Do I have to obey Momma?"

I said, "You are twenty-four years old. You certainly do not have to obey your mother!"

Now that will go over big with some people who claim they believe the Bible! They don't believe the Bible at all if that offends them. Children should be trained while they're children to obey their parents. But children should grow up and get out on their own. Parents should teach their children to make decisions for themselves. Parents are not responsible for their grown-up children.

I told this young couple to go ahead and get married. I said, "You are not being disrespectful toward your mother. She can't run your life and tell you what to do."

This was a situation between two Spirit-filled Christians, one of whom had been in the ministry for several years. We all prayed and were convinced that she had the same burden for ministry that he had. She had a desire to help him. I said, "You have to follow God then. I can't help what your mother said. I encourage you to follow what you believe God has said to both of you."

They went ahead and got married. Her parents didn't even come to the wedding. I marched down the aisle with her. Later, the mother and father said to them, "Will you forgive us? We were wrong. If we had to do it over again, we would be at your wedding."

The wife is to be the queen, or the head, of the home. Now the man is the head of the wife, but she is the head of the home. Let me give you a scripture. Inspired by the Spirit of God, Paul writes to Timothy, the pastor of a New Testament Church, and says, *"I will therefore that the younger women marry, bear children, GUIDE THE HOUSE, give none occasion to the adversary to speak reproachfully"* (1 Tim. 5:14).

The *King James Version* says, "guide the house," but the Greek actually says, "rule the household." That doesn't mean that the wife is to rule her husband. It means that the wife is to rule the household. It's not necessarily so in our modern-day households, but in the past, the woman was at the home all the time. Someone had to run the home while the husband was at work.

God's ideal for marriage is that every woman be queen in her home, that her home should be her empire. And her husband and children are her beloved subjects. It is to be a love kingdom. It is a historical fact that no nation rises above its homes. And no home rises above its motherhood. Genesis 3:20 says, *"And Adam called his wife's name Eve; because she was the mother of all living."*

A Christian Should Marry Another Christian

Does a believer have any right to marry an unbeliever? Second Corinthians 6:14 says, *"Be ye not unequally yoked together with unbelievers: for what fellowship hath righteousness with unrighteousness? and what communion hath light with darkness?"* The Christian who marries one from the world marries one from another family—those ruled by Satan. Three things happen as a result: The Christian *forfeits his freedom, limits his fellowship with God,* and *puts himself under bondage to the world.* I do not believe that is the will of God.

I remember a lady in our church who was one of the most spiritual women I had ever met. She was more spiritual

than any five preachers I knew or any five you could mention. She had the gifts of the Spirit operating in her life.
Now she wasn't a minister of the Gospel, but the Holy Spirit
operated through her marvelously.

When she got saved and filled with the Holy Spirit, she
and her husband were already married and had a family. I
think their youngest child was not yet born at that time. Her
husband was a good man; she loved him, and he loved her.
He provided for their home and would go to church with
her some. He was a good, law-abiding citizen who made a
living for them. He just wasn't interested in the things of
God. She went right on serving God. And when she was
fifty-five years old, he died. He did get saved before he died.
Thank God, he saw reality in her, and she got him saved.

Well, after she had been a widow for about five years, we
moved away for a couple of years, and then the Lord sent us
back to that church. In the meantime, we heard that she had
remarried. So when we moved back, we were straightening
things up in the parsonage, and one of her daughters—actually,
her oldest daughter who was about thirty-six years of age—came
to the parsonage to help us unpack boxes.

So my wife said to her, "We heard that your mother
remarried."

She said, "Yes, she has." You could tell she wasn't too
enthused about it. And so, we asked her about her mother.
Because we'd been gone for two years, we didn't know the
man she'd married. Actually, her mother and new husband
didn't live there. Her mother had gone to work in another
city before she ever met him.

So, finally, the daughter said, "Brother and Sister Hagin,
I'm sure that Momma missed God. She moved away about
a year after you both left. She went away to work and met
this man in the city she moved to. Then she brought him

here to introduce him to us children. And I just said to her, 'Momma, you aren't about to marry this guy, are you?'"

She said, "Well, yeah, I'm sure thinking about it."

"All of us children told her that we didn't think she ought to marry him. Now I didn't know the man at the time. I had only laid eyes on him once, but just being around him, I wasn't sure if he was a Christian or not. I didn't want to judge him, but I needed to know, so I asked my mom."

She said, "Well, he belongs to such-and-such church."

I said, "Momma, you know that everyone who belongs to a church is not saved. Church membership doesn't save a person. Besides that, he looks to me like he's an old beer-guzzler."

She said, "He does drink a little, but he said he'd quit if I married him."

Older women can be just as naive as younger women. It doesn't matter how spiritual you are. This woman was very spiritual. She had the gifts of the Spirit operating through her, but she was not listening to her spirit. A person can get over into the flesh very easily.

Whether you're young or old, if the person you are marrying isn't going to quit doing something *before* you are married, then that person isn't going to quit *after* you are married! And if you don't like the person just as he or she is, then you better forget it, because you're not going to change that person.

Someone once said that men marry women thinking they're going to remain just like they are for the rest of their life, and that women marry men thinking they're going to change them. Both of them wind up disappointed.

Well, her mother decided that she was going to fast and pray about it. You know, there's a danger sometimes in

79

fasting and praying, especially when the Bible already provides the answer that you need. And her daughter said to her, "Momma, the Bible said to be married only in the Lord. The Bible said not to be unequally yoked together with unbelievers [see 2 Cor. 6:14]. And if you'll obey the Bible, we are 100 percent for you! But if you won't obey the Bible, you're going to get in trouble."

Her mother still decided to fast and pray about it. Well, all her fasting and praying was not going to change the Bible. It's dangerous to fast and pray apart from the Word, because you throw yourself wide open. There are many spirits out there.

Remember, this woman had the gifts of the Spirit operating in her life—the word of wisdom and the word of knowledge. But in this situation, she just simply let her flesh, the natural person, dominate her. And there was some kind of spirit that spoke to her. You can know the Holy Spirit and still listen to wrong spirits. She said that the Lord told her to marry him.

So her daughter said, "I know that Momma made a mistake. I haven't heard anything from them. They have only been married now about three of four months."

That same week that she was talking to us and helping us straighten things up, we noticed a woman walking down the street. My wife said, "You know, that looks like Sister _____ walking this way."

I looked and said, "She sure does walk like her, but she doesn't live in this town. She lives in another city now."

We watched her, and as she got within a block of the parsonage, we noticed that it was her! I said, "I believe she's coming down here to the parsonage."

Now we haven't seen her in almost two years. So we rushed out of the parsonage to greet her. And by the time we hit the yard, we could see that her eye was black, and her nose was bruised. She looked like she had been run through a gristmill. Then she started crying and bawling.

We got her up on the parsonage porch, and my wife and I put our arms around her to comfort her. We asked her, "What's the matter?"

"About 11 or 12 days ago, my husband came in from work in the afternoon. He had been drinking, and I said something he didn't like. He just hit me right in the face and knocked me down. He jumped right in the middle of me and started beating me in the face. He almost beat me to death. Finally, I got loose from him. I rode a streetcar across the city to one of my daughters' house. I have been in bed for the last 10 days."

Well, our hearts went out to her. She said, "I'll tell you one thing. When I get up to Heaven, I have some questions I'm going to ask."

I said, "What are you going to ask God?"

She said, "I'm going to ask Him why He put this off on me."

I said, "Sister, you know me. I was your pastor here. I'm not trying to be smart, but there's no use in waiting to get to Heaven to ask Him. You can ask me now, and I'll tell you.

"God didn't put this off on you," I continued. "He didn't have a thing in the world to do with you marrying that old drinking geek. You just wanted him and so you got him. What are you going to do with him?"

I actually told her that! You see, good Christian people—Spirit-filled Christians, people with gifts of the Spirit operating in their lives—can miss God if they choose not to obey what the Word of God says. It was all right for her to marry again, but only in the Lord.

I've heard young women say, "Yeah, but I love him. I've found Mr. Right." But on the other hand, he wasn't saved.

They'd respond, "Oh, no. He's not a Christian. I'm going to get him saved, though. I'm just going to believe God."

Well, I noticed that this woman who married this unsaved man believed God and made all the right confessions. And it didn't turn out right. Now if she had listened to what the Bible told her in the first place, she wouldn't have been in the mess she was in.

Eventually, the man she married was running around with every woman in the country. He was not faithful to her. He was lying, cheating, and stealing. The law was after him, and he was on the run.

Children of the devil are going to act like the devil. They can't help it. We're not criticizing them; that's just their nature. The devil is their spiritual father. That's what Jesus said to the Pharisees (see John 8:44). They were very religious, the strictest sect of the Jewish religion. And yet, Jesus said they were of their father the devil. He didn't mean their physical father; he meant their spiritual father.

We inherit a natural, fleshly nature from our mother and father. But we've got a spiritual nature on the inside, and it's either of God or the devil. Even if our spirit is born again, our flesh will still want to do a lot of things that we shouldn't do. That's why Paul said, "I keep under my body" (1 Cor. 9:27).

We don't have to let the flesh dominate. We can let the love of God dominate us. Notice what it says in First Corinthians.

1 CORINTHIANS 7:27–28

27 *Art thou bound unto a wife? seek not to be loosed. Art thou loosed from a wife? seek not a wife.*

28 *But and if thou marry, thou hast not sinned; and if a virgin marry, she hath not sinned. Nevertheless such shall have TROUBLE IN THE FLESH: but I spare you.*

Paul is talking about two Christians having trouble in the flesh. Well, if you're hooked up with a spouse who is not saved, you're going to have *double* trouble in the flesh!

Remember that whatever happened to you in the past, you must forget. Start working on God's ideal for marriage now. If you haven't married yet, then learn what the Word of God says and be sure you enter into marriage according to Scripture.

Choosing a Mate

Now that we have established that it's God's will for a Christian to marry only another Christian, let's look at other important aspects in choosing a mate. People should not enter into marriage lightly. It should be a solemn and sacred thing.

One time my wife and I were holding a meeting in Houston, Texas. We didn't have any services on Saturday, so my wife and I decided to go over to another pastor's house for barbecue. I had held a meeting in his church a year or two before, and he wanted to discuss the possibility of me coming back to hold a meeting in his church.

While we were at his home visiting, a young lady in his congregation was there. She wanted us to know that she was getting married. She was so thrilled. So I asked, "Who are you marrying?" She was marrying an evangelist. Both of them were Christians. Both of them were filled with the Holy Ghost and spoke with other tongues.

This evangelist had just held a revival in their church. They had gotten acquainted to some extent. But here's where people miss it: They hastily rush into marriage. I knew immediately on the inside of me that she shouldn't marry him. Some people might say, "Well, both of them are Christians." That's true, but there is the will of God in things.

A few minutes later, I whispered in my wife's ear and said, "You ought to talk to the pastor's wife. Get her to talk to that girl. That girl is missing God by marrying that fellow."

My wife said, "I sensed the same thing." She had the same witness in her spirit.

And so, she talked to this pastor's wife, and the pastor's wife said, "My husband and I have the same witness. I've talked to her a little bit, but I saw that she wasn't listening so I just shut up."

Well, she married him. She really didn't know that much about him. I don't suppose they knew each other for more than two or three months before they married. You need to go with a person long enough to find out about him or her.

And so, he became very jealous of her. He was allowing his physical nature to dominate him, instead of the nature of God inside him. He wouldn't even let her shake hands with any of the men in church meetings. Well, naturally, as an evangelist's wife, people were shaking hands with her and greeting her.

If they stayed in a motel, she was not permitted out of the room. He wouldn't let her out of his sight for a second. She couldn't go to the store to get anything. And if some little thing went wrong, he would start breaking up furniture. He was very high-tempered and never learned to control himself. He was a big fellow and just knocked her around.

She stood it for as long as she could, but then her nerves were gone. She just couldn't live under that kind of pressure. She had no other choice; she had to leave him to preserve her health. She couldn't live in that kind of circumstance. No one could for long.

Well, he didn't make it in ministry. He wasn't living for God like he should have been. Even though he was a preacher, he was not in fellowship with God. A fellow who loses his temper, cusses, breaks up furniture, and knocks his

wife around is not in fellowship with God! He's more in
fellowship with the devil than anyone.

I read something some time ago that I thought was very
helpful. The authors were discussing marriage and said,
"Find someone with an equal spiritual experience as you,
and then build a life together." If you get to know someone,
some things will eventually come out. If he or she has a jealous nature, it will show up. Find out as much as possible
about each other before you marry.

I remember another similar situation that happened in
the early years of my ministry. A beautiful young lady who
was marvelously talented to work for God got involved with
a man who said he was a Christian but was not. He just pre-
tended to be. When I was within 10 feet of him, though he
might be kneeling at the altar, I knew it was all fake and just
a put-on. Any person with any spiritual perception could
have noticed this. But some people are so gullible.

He had also been divorced. If you are considering marrying a divorced person, find out why that person got
divorced. If the person you are marrying was the instigator
of the divorce, you don't want to get involved with him or
her. You will end up helping that person reap the seeds he
or she has sown. Now if the person was an innocent party,
that's a different situation.

Well, in this particular situation, the man who this beautiful young lady was going to marry had deliberately left his
wife. But she didn't know that. She wasn't that close to him.
Several of us who were close to her knew in our spirits that
she shouldn't marry this fellow. But she wouldn't listen to
us. She just went her way.

Finally, I remember she was in a service and came to
the altar. Some of us prayed with her and let her know that
we loved her, because she had been out of church and out
of fellowship. As she knelt there at the altar, she said, "No,

I'm not going to marry him. It's not right. I'm not going to do it." We rejoiced with her decision. But it wasn't six weeks later that we found out she had gone ahead and married him.

Once she married, no one ever heard from her anymore. She never came to church. After many months, she finally wrote a letter to one of her closest friends who lived in the same town. She wrote, "Oh, my God! Why didn't I listen? I'm in hell! He's so jealous that he won't let me out of the house!"

She had to secretly write the letter and get someone else to mail it because he wouldn't let her out of his sight for a moment.

At one time, she had been a great singer for the Lord. She had the ability to speak. She could just hold a group of young people in her hand as she spoke to them. God could have used her mightily. But her husband sold her piano because he was jealous of her and her music. He took her guitar and beat it to pieces. Situations like this are so sad. We tried to tell her, but she wouldn't listen.

Can You Choose Any Mate You Want?

You can believe for everything the Word of God promises you or provides for you. You can't believe beyond it. That's where people get in trouble. Why can't you? Romans 10:17 says, *"So then faith comes by hearing, and hearing by the word of God."* Faith is based on what God's Word says. And you cannot believe out beyond the knowledge of God's Word.

For instance, several years ago, a denominational pastor received the Holy Spirit, spoke with other tongues, and was kicked out of his denomination. With no church to pastor, he went into business for himself in a large city and attended the largest Full Gospel church in the city. He was unattached, probably between thirty-five and forty years of age.

He told me that there was this beautiful lady who sang in the choir and since "you can have what you say," and "whatever you desire, just pray and believe you receive [Mark 11:24]," he was going to pray and believe that he received this beautiful lady as his wife.

But I can't read in the Bible where God's Word says, "I promise John that he can have Mary for a wife." Mary might not want to be his wife! And John might be just as well off without her anyhow!

I asked him, "Have you ever talked to this woman? Have you ever had a date with her?"

He said, "No. No."

Sitting out there in the congregation while the choir sang on Sunday morning, he had fastened his eyes upon her and was attracted to her. Since, "you can have what you say," he thought that if he said it, it would come to pass. Yes, but under what conditions would it come to pass? If he believed it strongly enough? No. Faith comes by hearing, and hearing by the Word of God (see Rom. 10:17). And the Word of God says, *"Whoso findeth a wife findeth a good thing, and obtaineth favour of the Lord"* (Prov. 18:22).

You see, you have to do something about it. The Lord will lead you and guide you. You have a right to claim guidance, because He has promised to guide you. You have a right to claim that He will lead you. But just to pick out someone and say, "I'm going to believe God and she's going to be my wife," is unscriptural.

Well now, she may not want to be your wife. Or, that would work the other way around. He may not want to be your husband. Where another person's will comes into play on the matter, friends, you're not going to be able to override his or her will. And you might as well settle that once and for all.

God Himself does not exercise authority over human spirits. If He did, He would make everyone in the whole world get saved today, and we would go on to be with the Lord. We have authority over evil spirits, *not* human spirits. God Himself does not exercise authority over human spirits; He lets people choose for themselves.

Believe God for a Mate

In the first meeting I held after leaving my last pastorate, a lady, in her thirties who had never married, said to me, "Brother Hagin, do I have the right to believe for a husband?"

"I believe so," I said, "because the Bible says, *'Whoso findeth a wife findeth a good thing, and obtaineth favour of the Lord'* [Prov. 18:22]. And it would be a poor rule that wouldn't work both ways.

"Now you can't just pick out someone and say, 'That one's mine.' But you can ask God to lead you. You can claim God's guidance by faith and let Him work it out because you believe Him."

I remember two beautiful young ladies in a revival meeting I conducted in Oklahoma. They had just graduated from high school with the highest grades in their class. They were saved and baptized in the Holy Spirit in that meeting.

After some time, I went back there for some teaching sessions. One of these young ladies, now about 20, was there and the Lord had me minister to her one night.

Afterwards, the pastor said, "Brother Hagin, I'm so glad you did that. You didn't know this, I'm sure, but she's engaged to be married to a young man, and we're concerned about it. He came in here, and I'll be honest with you, I'm sure he just made like he got saved so he could get her."

I hadn't known these details the night the Lord had me minister to her. She was sitting on the front seat. I told the congregation to sing, because I didn't want everyone to hear, and I said to her, "The Lord told me to tell you this, 'I've got something better for you. Don't marry right now. I've got something better for you.'"

Two years later I was out in California in a campmeeting. A young lady, along with a fine looking young man, came up to me and said, "Brother Hagin, do you remember me?"

"No," I said, "but your face looks familiar." She gave me her name, but I still couldn't remember.

"Well," she said, "you'll remember this. You called me up while the congregation was singing and told me the Lord said not to marry right now; He had something better for me."

"Oh," I said, "I remember that."

"Well," she said happily, "here he is!" Then she told me that she and her husband were in Bible college preparing for the ministry.

"Oh, I'm so glad," she said. "I would have made a fatal mistake. I'm so glad the Lord arrested me and ministered to me. We're so happy. And we're working for God." He did have something better for her.

You see, we can believe God and exercise faith for anything that is promised us in the Bible. *"So then faith cometh by hearing, and hearing by the Word of God"* (Rom. 10:17). Faith is based upon hearing what God's Word says.

When we get into areas beyond the Word, we get into gray areas, into dark areas. As long as you're in the Word, you're in the light; you're on safe and sure ground. And you can trust God for guidance. He has promised to guide you. You can claim guidance by faith. You can say, "The Lord is guiding me. He is leading me. I may not see it this moment. I may not even know what to do at the moment, but He is my guide, and I am trusting Him."

Romans 8:14 says, *"For as many as are led by the Spirit of God, they are the sons of God."* He will guide you, but remember that the Lord just leads you one step at a time.

The Problem of Divorce

I remember a particular family who within a two-year period of time was wiped out. They got a certain type of tuberculosis called "galloping consumption." I don't mean just the brothers and sisters died. I mean both sides of the family—everyone! It just went right through the family.

Divorce is just like that. It's a disease that will go right through a family. But, thank God, there's a cure. Christians themselves have to determine to walk in the light of God's Word. I don't lose my free will just because I become a Christian. I'm still a free moral agent; I still have a will of my own. I can will to serve God or not to serve God, even though I'm a Christian.

If you're walking in fellowship with God, you want to serve God. But if you get into a poor state of fellowship, then, of course, the flesh and the natural, human mind will take over and dominate you. The devil will take advantage of those opportunities. But people who walk in close fellowship with God want to please God. If people will get to God and walk in the light of His Word, divorce won't be a problem.

The Four Problems of Husbands and Wives

There are many books available on marriage. But the Bible is the best book on marriage there is! I have also learned a lot of things concerning marriage, divorce, and remarriage through practical experience, because I started pastoring in my late teens. I pastored for 12 years. And as a pastor, I had to deal with all kinds of family problems.

Additional insights I have received as a traveling minister have led me to the conclusion that the problems of husbands and wives typically center around four things: (1) *religion*, (2) *sex*, (3) *money*, and (4) *children*. One of the best ways to avoid problems in these four areas is to discuss them in detail before you get married.

Discuss Before Marriage

I didn't know a lot about marriage because I had never been taught anything. I never read a book on the subject. My daddy left when I was just a boy. I knew virtually nothing about sex or anything else concerning husband-and-wife relationships. But I read the Bible. And by listening to the Holy Ghost in my spirit, I had wisdom beyond myself. It wasn't me. I was walking in fellowship with God. When I proposed to my wife and she said, "Yes," I said to her, "Well, before we go any further, if we're old enough to be married, then we're old enough to talk about a few things."

We talked about religion first. I said to her, "Now, number one, I am a preacher." And she knew that. I said, "I have to go where God says to go. And if God says to go to Africa, then I have to go to Africa." She knew nothing about the ministry. She was not called to the ministry, but she would need to go along with me if she's my wife. And there are some things that could have come as a rude awakening if she didn't know about them ahead of time.

"I love you more than my momma or any other person on the earth," I told her. "But I don't love you more than I love Jesus. Jesus comes first with me. He ought to come first with you. But because Jesus comes first with me, I'm going to love you with the love of Jesus." And if Jesus comes first with the wife, then she's going to love her husband with the love of Jesus too.

I have come across preachers who were so miserable. God called them to be evangelists, so they have to be gone from home much of the time. But their wives rebel against that. The preachers decide to satisfy their wives instead. They became pastors, and, as a result, they are miserable all the time. There's misery in the home. There's no fellowship in the home. No wonder the children go off and serve the devil when they are brought up in that kind of environment. I was determined that this was not going to happen to my family and me.

Then I said, "If we're old enough to get married, we're old enough to talk about sex." Neither one of us knew anything about it.

I said, "You need to understand something about a man and his makeup. And I need to understand something about a woman." We got into agreement.

Then we discussed children. I asked, "Are we going to have any children?" We both agreed that we would. "How many are we going to have?"

My wife said, "Oh, we can settle all that after we're married."

"No," I said, "let's get it settled now, beforehand." My wife and I agreed that we'd have two children. We agreed that we would have a boy first and then a girl. We even talked about their names.

Finally, we discussed money. Well, we didn't have much to worry about back then! After we got married, we had two nickels left, and we used them to buy two candy bars. We decided that if we were going to start out, we might as well start out on the bottom. We couldn't go any other way but up!

I did say, "I know for one thing that I'll not be able at the present time to dress you like your daddy does." Because she was the only girl and the baby of the family, her dad bought her whatever she wanted. The price did not matter. I explained that there was a sacrifice to ministry. Paul said to Timothy, "Endure hardness as a good soldier of Jesus Christ" (2 Tim. 2:3).

We made our dedication together with the Lord. And there did come a time when she only had one dress that she could wear in public. And, really, it wasn't that good. But she never said a word. I also got down to the place where I only had one suit that I could wear. It was frayed around the collar, and the sleeves were practically worn out. But, eventually, we began to rise to the top.

You need to discuss these things before you get married. And if you're already married, then discuss these things now and get into agreement. If you're not in agreement, it will hinder your prayers. Look in First Peter chapter 3.

1 PETER 3:7

> 7 *Likewise, ye husbands, dwell with them according to knowledge, giving honour unto the wife, as unto the weaker vessel, and as being heirs together of the grace of life; that YOUR PRAYERS BE NOT HINDERED.*

We do a lot of preaching on faith and prayer, but whatever hinders your prayers will hinder your faith. Prayer and faith go together. If you don't give honor to your spouse, your prayers will be hindered.

#1 Religion

The number one problem in marriages is religion. A believer shouldn't marry an unbeliever. The Bible says, *"Be ye not unequally yoked together with unbelievers . . ."* (2 Cor. 6:14). Then in so many cases, neither the husband nor the wife are Christians when they get married. But afterwards, one of them gets saved. Remember Paul covers that in First Corinthians 7:12–16.

If the unbeliever is pleased to dwell with the Christian, that's fine. But if the unbeliever is running around committing adultery and is not pleased to dwell with the Christian spouse, then let the unbeliever depart. Each situation must be looked at in light of the law of love.

I remember in one church that I pastored, we had a little redheaded woman. She wasn't very big or very tall. Her husband was a great big fellow who weighed about two hundred and forty pounds. I didn't know anything about their background, just that the woman was saved and the husband wasn't saved. He was always running around, gambling and drinking.

94

Because we lived in a small town, everyone knew everything about everyone. People in the church said that before she got saved and baptized with the Holy Spirit, she was just as bad as he was. She would cuss louder than he would. And she would fight her husband who weighed two hundred and forty pounds and would whip him! She would pick up an iron skillet and knock him in the head.

They had been married several years and had three or four children. She brought her children to Sunday school and church, but her husband never came. Finally, one time at the breakfast table, her husband asked, "Why don't you just move your bed up there to that church? You stay up at that church more than you do at home!"

She said, "Honey, you know that's not so. I'm up there Wednesday night, Sunday morning, and Sunday night. But even if I was at home, you're not here. You're gone every night. I make sure that your meals are all ready and that the house is clean."

He responded, "Yeah, you just might as well move your bed up there!"

He made plenty of money, because he had a good job with a good company, but he gambled it all away. They lived way beneath where they could have lived if he had conserved his money. But instead, he just wasted it.

She only had one pair of shoes. He thought he would put a stop to her going to church, so he threw her shoes up in the attic. She didn't know where he hid them. She couldn't find her shoes, and he thought, *Well, she won't go to church now.* But instead, she just put her galoshes on and went to church anyway.

My wife asked me, "Did you see Sister Sylvia's feet?"

I said, "No! I didn't notice her feet! Was there something wrong with her feet?" I did notice that she had a glow on her face. She just seemed to shine.

My wife said, "She had galoshes on."

Later this redheaded woman said to her husband, teasingly, "If you don't like me the way I am, I believe I'll just go back to being the way I used to be." Well, he remembered how she used to be.

He said, "Oh, no! Oh, no!" Even though he weighed two hundred and forty pounds, like I said, he didn't like it when she got mad while she was cooking. She would pick up her iron skillet full of hot grease and knock him in the head!

"No!" he said, "I like you a whole lot better like you are. You stay just the way you are!"

She said, "Well, you are the head of this family, because you are the husband. You should take the spiritual lead, but you're not saved. When we sit down at the table, you start eating like a hog. We ought to pray before we eat. I pray with our children and take them to Sunday school and church. But we ought to pray as a family."

He said, "Well, all right, you go ahead and pray." So they started having prayer at the table.

Then she said to him, "Now we ought to have a time of Bible reading in the home too. You ought to do it. You ought to take the lead in reading the Bible and praying."

He said, "You go ahead and do it." So they began to have a time of Bible reading and prayer in the home.

This is a perfect example of a problem concerning religion within a marriage. He's not saved, and she is. There's a division between the two of them. And there's a great pull between the children. If the children are not Christians, they will usually follow the natural instead of the spiritual. This in turn can cause all kinds of problems.

Another example of a potential problem concerning religion is when one spouse is of one denomination and the other spouse is of another denomination. For example, if one spouse is Methodist and the other spouse is Baptist, it may create great problems if both parties are stubborn and unwilling to work with the other person. Now, of course, if folks are really saved and born again, they will walk in the law of love. That will make a big difference!

I remember one particular man who was saved, but his wife wasn't. They had a farm which was paid for and they had all the equipment they needed. They also had a home full of brand-new furniture. After this man got saved, he wanted to pay his tithes. But his wife had a fit. She said, "No, you're not!" Soon after, they had a cotton-crop failure and wound up losing everything.

Some time later, he started coming to church again. He rededicated his life to God. That was in August. At the end of September, his first bale of cotton came in. He brought his tithes to the church.

He said, "This time my wife insisted. She said, 'Don't forget your tithes.' She remembered losing everything." Finally, after three or four months, she came to church, got under conviction, came down to the altar, and got saved.

Now, you see, all of this was over religion. She didn't like his religion. They lost everything they had. But, thank God, they started paying their tithes, and God began to bless them.

When I lived in Garland, Texas, there was a young man who was saved and filled with the Holy Ghost. He was active in youth work. He met a young lady there in the church who was also saved and filled with the Holy Ghost. They got married.

Now when they married, this young man was a "lay preacher." He would go out on weekends once in a while and preach for someone. But he wouldn't be gone every weekend. After they had been married a few years, he was going out pretty regularly. He had developed into a good evangelist. So he decided to resign his job and preach full time, because he was almost gone full time anyway. He was preaching every weekend.

His wife said, "I'm not going! I didn't marry a preacher!"

He said, "Yes, you did. I was preaching when you married me."

"Well, yeah, but I thought you would never do any more than what you'd been doing. I'm not going! If you're going, you can go without me. I'm going to stay right here. I want a home and a life like others," she said.

People get in trouble when they try to be like other people. They ought to want to be like Jesus. Well, she stayed, and he went. And, of course, it wasn't but two years later that she found another man.

As a divorced man, as long as this evangelist stayed single, he could keep credentials with his particular group, but if he ever remarried, they would take his credentials. It was a sad situation. They should have talked about these things and reached an agreement before they were married.

#2 Sex

The number two problem in marriages is sex. Many times religion and sex are mixed together. For example, sometimes a woman gets so "spiritual" that she won't go to bed with her husband. She doesn't want her husband to touch her. He may be saved and even baptized with the Holy Spirit, but he's not spiritual enough in her eyes. And in a very few cases, the same is true with the husband.

I was holding a meeting for a young man. He got saved under my ministry as a 15-year-old boy. Now he was an ordained minister and had two children. But he became so "spiritual" that he didn't want to sleep with his wife. She was more sexually passionate than he was. She wanted to sleep with him, and ought to have been able to, because his body is not just his; it's hers also.

So I had to talk to both of them. I said to the husband, "You're going to have to pull up, and she's going to have to pull back. You're going to have to find a happy medium. You're going to have to meet together because if you don't take care of her, someone else just might."

They didn't listen. And some time later, he came in and found another man in bed with his wife. The fact that his wife's sexual appetite was not being satisfied in no way justifies her actions. She was still responsible for her own moral behavior. However, because she was not getting her sexual needs met, it made her more vulnerable, or more susceptible, to temptation.

In August of 1943, I was holding a church meeting in east Texas. The pastor of the church and I decided to attend a fellowship meeting in another church nearby. They only had night services in this particular revival. And some of the officials of this particular Full Gospel denomination asked me to preach at their fellowship meeting, so I did.

We had dinner there on the grounds. Afterwards, the pastor and one of the officials of the denomination came up to me and asked if I would go with them to pray for one of the ladies in his church because she was having fainting spells. And so I consented to go.

The lady's home was right up the hill, not too far from the meeting place. You could almost see the house from the church, because it sat right on top of the hill. Now both husband and wife were saved and members of that church. The husband had never received the baptism of the Holy Ghost, but the wife had received the baptism of the Holy Ghost and was a Sunday school teacher in the church.

She had been having these spells for some time. They would pray for her, and she would get better. And then, she would just pass out. If she were in the living room, she would just pass out on the couch. They thought she might have a demon. They asked me to come along so that I could detect if she had a demon and cast it out of her, because I'd had some success along that line.

When we walked into the house, she was lying on the couch. She was moaning and carrying on. I observed for a moment, looked on the inside of me, and said to the husband, "Get me a glass of water." So he went and got a big goblet full of water and handed it to me. Then I threw the water in her face. She jumped up in a hurry.

I said, "Now, sister, just get up from there. There's nothing in the world wrong with you. It's not even the devil. All in the world that's wrong with you is that you think you've gotten so 'spiritual' that you won't have anything to do with your husband. So you're feigning these sick spells to keep from having sex with him." That was exactly what it was. That's a dangerous thing to do.

I knew another woman who was in her mid-thirties, and the doctors couldn't find anything wrong with her. The minute I walked into her presence, the Spirit of God said to me, "She doesn't want to have anything to do with her husband. She's not sick." But this lady wouldn't accept that and do anything about it.

Two or three years later, she got an incurable disease and was bedfast for several years. She got that disease because she was feigning something. She opened the door for the devil. If she had settled the issue in the light of the Word of God, she would have been so much better off.

Can a person be truly spiritual without obeying the Bible? Why, certainly not! Let's look at what First Corinthians 7:5 says: *"Defraud ye not one the other, except it be with consent for a time, that ye may give yourselves to fasting and prayer; and come together again, that Satan tempt you not for your incontinency."* The Greek literally reads, "Withhold not sexual intercourse from one another, except it be by consent [both of you consent to it], that you may give yourself to fasting and prayer and then come together again, lest Satan tempt you because of your incontinency [failure to restrain sexual appetite]."

In 1949, I left the last church that I pastored. I then went out on the field from 1949 to 1962 and part of 1963. In other words, I was in field ministry for 13 or 14 years. I was primarily in the churches in what we called "church meetings."

Now the majority of the time, I stayed in various church parsonages with the pastor and his wife. I held a lot of meetings during that span of time. I would usually only take Christmas week off. Sometimes that's the only week in the whole year I would take off. I might take off a day or two to travel, but I was on the road ministering constantly.

So you can imagine how many places I preached and how many pastors I preached for. Over the course of time, I gathered statistics and made a few polls of my own. I noticed a problem back then that is still a major problem today.

Many of the pastors I talked to had sex problems. Sometimes the husband would talk to me, and sometimes both he and his wife would talk to me. They would say, "Brother Hagin, could we talk to you?" I learned a lot about people by just being in their homes and their seeking my counsel.

Birth Control

One time while I was staying with a pastor in his apartment, he woke me up early in the morning. He was crying. This twenty-eight-year-old pastor was crying. His wife and two children had packed up all their stuff, gotten in the car, and left him.

So I said, "We'll pray."

He said, "You don't know my wife. She's hardheaded."
I didn't say anything, but I thought, *If she's as hardheaded as him, no wonder they have trouble.* Two hardheads are butting each other, like two billy goats.

I said, "She'll be back. We will agree."

He said, "I'm ashamed to get up and tell anyone, you know?"

I said, "Well, don't tell anyone. You don't have to go around broadcasting that your wife left you. She'll be back. I'll say this by faith: She'll be back in three days." And three days later, she returned.

I went down to the parsonage and got them together. I never saw a woman so mad in all my life. Now, in some ways, she had a right to be mad. She thought I was taking sides with him, so she started yelling at him. Soon, they were yelling at each other. Their faces were red! I had to get louder than them and scream, "Shut up!"

I pointed my finger right in their faces and pushed them down in a chair and said, "I command you to shut up in the Name of Jesus."

The wife was trembling all over. I said to her, "Now I want you to know something. I'm not on his side. [There are usually three sides to every argument: The husband's side, the wife's side, and the right side.] I can already see where he's wrong. We're going to straighten him out. But at the same time, I am going to try to straighten you out."

I didn't know anything about what I was supposed to do. I just knew the Bible. I gave each one of them a sheet of paper and a pencil. I said, "Make two columns. Write down all the good things about your spouse on one side and all the bad things about your spouse on the other side." They calmed down and began writing. I noticed that the good part was twice as long as the bad part. I said, "Let's work on the bad parts."

I decided to take up his complaint first. His number one complaint concerned sex; she didn't want him to touch her. So I said to the wife, "Why don't you want him to touch you?"

"We have two children, and I have had an awful time both times in labor. I don't want any more children. And he doesn't want to use any preventative measures."

"I don't blame you. You're right. Don't let him touch you," I said.

I turned to the husband and said, "You're wrong. You're griping about the fact that she doesn't want you to touch her. Well, I don't blame her. Now birth control is not wrong."

Then she said, "We've been married all these years, and I love my husband. I want to go to bed with him. I'm just about as sexually active as he is. But I start thinking about getting pregnant, and it's all over for me."

"Well," I said, "he ought to protect you. It's his job to take the lead."

I said to the husband, "You should protect her; do something about this."

She said, "If I'm not going to get pregnant, I'll go to bed with him every night!" So we just took each item on the list and got it straightened out. But as I said before: Many people I've talked to have had sex problems.

Selfish Men

A common complaint of many men has been the following: "My wife is cold and frigid. She won't have anything to do with me."

I usually tell them, "There isn't any such thing as a cold and frigid woman. They don't exist. The only thing that exists is an ignorant, stupid, fumbling, bungling man."

This is where the problem is. Man is just interested in himself and his own satisfaction. He's selfish. He's not interested in his wife. He's not interested in what pleases her. But love always puts the other person first. I'm always concerned about putting my wife first. I'm not interested in *getting* something; I'm interested in *giving* something in life. "Love seeketh not its own" (1 Cor. 13:5).

If you don't know about some of these things, you can get a good Christian book on the subject of sex and then work on it. It won't just happen. Some people think that it will just come naturally. No, you've got to work on it. A good sex life is a healthy life. God intended for it to be that way. It will pay off for you physically, mentally, and spiritually. Sex in marriage is a good, clean thing. It is a God-ordained thing. Paul said, "Marriage is honorable, and the marriage bed is undefiled" (Heb. 13:4).

I remember one fellow who was sleeping in one bedroom, and his wife was sleeping in another bedroom. He was thirty-two years old, and he said that he was never going to touch his wife again. He said that she was as cold as an iceberg. Who wants to get in bed with an iceberg?

I said to him, "Now that's not going to work. You're just a young man like I am. The Bible says not to withhold sexual intercourse from one another, because if you do, Satan will tempt you in this area [1 Cor. 7:5]. Another woman will approach you or something will happen, and you'll be more vulnerable; you'll be more likely to fall. Your ministry will be ruined. The church will split. This is not going to work."

He said, "Well, she's the coldest woman I've ever seen in my life. She's just frigid."

"There's no such thing as a frigid woman. They don't exist. The only thing that exists is an inept man who doesn't know anything. Your wife isn't cold—you're just stupid!" I said.

He said, "Yeah, but you don't know my wife."

I said, "I don't know your wife, but I'll guarantee you that she's not frigid. The problem is with you! Are you affectionate toward her? Do you court her? Or are you just interested in having sex?" All he did was have sex. He was just interested in satisfying himself, and that was the end of it.

"You need to hold her in your arms," I replied. "She's your wife. Kiss her. Tell her how much you love her. Do you ever do that?"

"No," he said.

I realized he did not understand how to be a friend to his wife, how to listen to her and focus on meeting her needs. He did not understand the importance of affection and many other things, so I gave him a Christian book on sex to read, and I left.

About a month later, I was in his part of the country so I decided to drive by and see he and his wife one afternoon. I drove up their driveway and parked. I sounded the horn, but no one came out. I sounded the horn again, and then, I finally sounded it a third time. I thought they were gone. I started to drive away when their front door opened.

When he came out, he looked a little disheveled. I said, "What's the matter with you?"

"Brother Hagin, you were right! You gave me that book, and things have really changed. Now my wife wants to go to bed with me, sometimes twice a day!"

I said, "You've been married ever since she was 19, and she has never had any benefit or satisfaction in the marriage. She's trying to make up for the last 14 years! Go back in there and take care of her." He learned something. They stayed together and have been successful in marriage and ministry.

Be Honest With Your Spouse

Another problem in marriage could have been solved by discussing it ahead of time. I remember two RHEMA students who got married after they graduated. They had been married a year and still hadn't had sex. The husband couldn't have an erection. Why didn't he tell her that before they were married? This is something they should have discussed before marriage.

I remember a young evangelist who wound up on the "spiritual junk heap" because of this same problem. This young man got married when he was about twenty-five years old. He was one of the leading evangelists in his state. He and his wife sang together.

They had been married six months, and the wife approached her pastor's wife and said, "How long were you both married before you had sex?"

The pastor's wife said, "It was the first night."

This young woman said, "We've been married six months, and he hasn't said or done anything; he hasn't approached me in any way." That marriage didn't last. They could have had the marriage legally annulled, because they never really consummated the marriage. She stayed with him for 18 months and then left. Who wants a marriage like that?

My wife and I discussed sex before we were married. We were very honest with one another. I let her know ahead of time what I expected from the standpoint of sex, and she communicated openly with me also. We came to a mutually acceptable agreement.

Our marriage and sex life have been wonderful because we got started off right. And we've stayed with it. We agreed that we would always be sweethearts. And after more than sixty years, we're still sweethearts. She goes to sleep every night in my arms. The last thing she says before she goes to sleep is, "I love you." The last thing I say is, "I love you."

We both say, "I love you" first thing in the morning, and then we kiss one another. We do the same thing every morning. I let her know how much I love and appreciate her. And she lets me know how much she loves and appreciates me. Marriage is beautiful.

Some years ago, my wife and I were counseling a couple. My wife asked them if they ever said, "I love you" to one another. They were always fighting. The wife had never shown any affection toward her husband. So my wife worked her over real good. She asked her, "Do you really love him?"

She said, "Oh, yes, I love him."

"Do you ever *tell* him you love him?"

"No," she said.

"Do you ever kiss him?"

"No," she said.

"Does he ever kiss you?"

She said, "Well, he wants to sometimes."

There was definitely something wrong here. Now I'm sure that they both loved each other from a natural standpoint; otherwise, they never would have gotten married. But they were not walking in divine love. They were not walking in the light of the Word of God.

A Domineering Woman

In 1945 my wife and I held a meeting in west Texas. We stayed with the pastor and his wife. Every time I asked the pastor a question, his wife would answer. We noticed that she ran everything. She played the piano for the church, and someone else led the singing. When the praise and worship was over, she left; she didn't stay for church. She went downtown to the drugstore for a cold drink.

She told me, "Now when I come back in, you close." I never paid any attention to her. The Holy Ghost is supposed to run the service, not the pastor's wife. So I just didn't pay any attention to her. She wanted everything her way.

Now we were sitting down for dinner one night. She sat at the head of the table instead of her husband. She started talking and didn't stop. I just kept my mouth shut. I didn't want any confrontation. She was talking about a situation involving a certain woman, which I didn't agree with. She wanted me to agree with her. Well, I didn't want to start a fuss in their home at their table. So I just simply said, "Go ahead, sister."

She said, "Now that's right, Brother Hagin, isn't it? You're a Bible teacher. You ought to know."

I said, "You're doing the talking. Go ahead. I'm just listening."

She went on talking, just blabbing away. She never gave anyone a chance to say anything. Her husband sat there and never said a word. He just looked embarrassed.

Again, she said, "Now that's right, Brother Hagin, isn't it?"

I said, "You're doing the talking; I'm just doing the listening."

The third time, she said, "Brother Hagin, that's right, isn't it? You agree with that, don't you?"

I didn't agree with it. The Bible doesn't agree with it. And any intelligent person wouldn't agree with it. I simply said to her, "Sister, I'm not talking. You're doing the talking. Just go ahead; I'm listening."

Finally, the fourth time, she said, "Now that's right; you *know* that's right. I want you to speak. Tell me whether you think that's right or not. I know you're bound to. Just speak up."

So I said, "No, it's not right. I tried to avoid the confrontation, but you just kept on. It's not right. I don't agree with it. The Bible doesn't agree with it. It's not scriptural."

Now there were big goblets full of iced tea sitting on the table. When I didn't agree with her, she picked up her goblet of tea and threw it across the table in my face. She was as mad as an old wet hen. I started laughing. And in love, I picked up my glass and threw the tea in her face. Then she picked up her husband's glass and threw the tea the length of the table, right in my face. She ruined all the food. I was laughing the whole time. I picked up my wife's glass and threw it back in her face. She picked up her son's glass, and when she did, I picked up the tea pitcher. Then she set the glass down. I was laughing. I didn't hate her; she was just wrong.

Let me show you how wrong she was. We concluded the meeting and then the next week, she and her husband were going to the mountains of New Mexico. They invited us to go with them. Before we left on this trip, the husband and I started talking. He said to me, "You know, my wife will run around all day long, and when she knows it's about time for me to come home, she'll get in bed. She'll put a wet cloth on her head and start moaning like something's wrong with her.

"Brother Hagin, you may get tired of me saying, 'I'll have to ask my wife.' You may get tired of that, but I just have to in order to get along with her. I go about three or four months at a time without sex. But when I bring her to the mountains, she lets me have sex with her once."

I said, "Dear God, she's just a prostitute. She's selling it." That is absolutely the truth. So we all went to the mountains. He got to have sex. Now that's sad, but true!

My wife and I talked about it. They were pastoring a church, and he was just a young man at the time. He could be tempted. And if he did fall, he would not be the only one to blame; *she* would be at fault also.

There is one thing I can say on her behalf. Years later, I met them again at a Voice of Healing Convention in Philadelphia. She held on to my hand and began to cry. She said, "Brother Hagin, I want you to forgive me. I was so selfish and wrong. I wronged my husband. Isn't it terrible that someone has to live to be nearly fifty years old before they learn any sense?"

I said, "Well, it sure is."

"But, thank God, I learned. Now I'm a wife to my husband. Things are better. God has blessed us, and we've started another church in another place. It is just thriving." You see, she wasn't running it; the Holy Ghost was running it now.

A Memory of the Past

I was holding a meeting in south Texas in the largest Full Gospel church in the town. Every night after I finished my message and ministered to the sick, a young lady would come to the altar and cry her heart out. She cried like someone does when there has been a tragedy.

I picked up my Bible and notebook and stepped down off the platform. She was kneeling at the end of the altar, and, as I went by her, I simply said to myself, *Lord, bless this young lady.* I felt so sorry for her. My heart went out to her.

The next night the same thing happened. She came up to the altar and cried so hard that I thought her heart would break. I walked by her again and said, "Lord, bless this dear lady." I could see that she was in some kind of difficulty.

So the third night, as I walked by her, I asked the Lord what was wrong with her. And just as fast as I can snap my finger, I knew the whole thing. I knew exactly what was wrong with her. So I went to the pastor who was visiting with people after the service and said, "Is that young lady a member of your church?"

The pastor said, "Yes, she's a member here. She's only been saved about a month."

"Do you know what's wrong with her?" I asked.

The pastor asked me, "Do you?"

I said, "I sure do."

He said, "Tell me."

So I said, "She's been married for two years, but she and her husband have never consummated the marriage. They've never had sex. She's divorcing him because she thought it wasn't fair to him.

"When she was nine years old, she came home from school and found her mother in bed with another man. She loves her husband, and they can be very loving. But when they start to have sex, that vision of her mother in bed with another man flashes before her, and she starts screaming."

"Why, Brother Hagin," the pastor said, "you're exactly right. My wife and I have stayed up until two and three in the morning talking to her, trying to help her. Can you help her?"

I said, "I know exactly how to help her." The Holy Spirit will not show you something about people without showing you how to help them.

So I began to talk to her. I showed her what the Bible said about it. I said to her, "Now it was wrong for your mother to be in bed with another man, but it's not wrong for you to be in bed with your husband." I spoke with her some more and gave her a little book that I thought would help.

I went back 15 months later, and the pastor said to me, "Do you remember the little lady you talked to last year?" I did remember her and the situation.

He said, "Well, her husband got saved and filled with the Holy Ghost. They just had a new baby boy. They named him Kenneth." Knowing what God's Word says and then acting on it saved their marriage.

In discussing the subject of sex, you have to remember that divine love is behind it all. *"Love worketh no ill to his neighbor . . ."* (Rom. 13:10). I've always put my wife first in everything. When I'm home, I always cook breakfast for her.

If we are eating bacon and eggs, I always give her the best pieces of bacon and the best eggs. I put her first in every area of life.

When it comes to sex, I find out what she wants, not what I want. What will satisfy her? You will find that if you and your spouse try to outdo one another in love, you will have Heaven on earth.

#3 Money

The number three problem in marriages is money. There was a couple who came to RHEMA Bible Training Center, and who were having financial problems. The husband didn't know a thing about managing money, and I don't think the wife knew much, either. If he wanted something, he would just buy it. They accumulated huge credit card bills over a period of time and were being charged 20 percent interest. Both of them were working, but all their money was gone. They didn't have any wisdom in this area.

She resented the fact that he went out and bought whatever he wanted to. So they talked about it, and he agreed to do better. But then, he went out and bought something else.

They decided to see a money counselor who told them to consolidate all of their bills so they would only have one payment a month. They did that and ended up with a payment that was much cheaper. They finally had enough money to live on.

Now that all the credit cards were free, what did he do? He went out and charged on all the credit cards again. That's ignorance gone to seed.

So many times, people want to blame the devil. But it's not the devil; it's just a lack of wisdom and good sense. The Bible says, *"If any of you lack wisdom, let him ask of God, that giveth to all men liberally, and upbraideth not; and it shall be given him"* (James 1:5).

You have to operate within your means. If you don't have the money, don't buy it. You can see that financial issues can create a lot of problems within a marriage. Both of these people were working full-time and still didn't have enough money for food. That's not wisdom.

John Wesley, founder of the Methodist church, said, "Make all you can; save all you can; and give all you can." But many people don't have any savings at all, and if an emergency comes along, it just knocks them for a loop.

I remember a lady who worked for us. She turned her paycheck over to her husband, and he handled their finances. She received a good salary, but didn't know where any of her money was going. Unfortunately, her husband wasn't very responsible and didn't spend the money where it ought to be spent.

As partners, they both should know where the money is going. In fact, she was making more money than he was. She was more equipped and skilled than he was to handle their finances. She thought everything was fine, because he never said anything. She just turned her check over to him.

Then one day, they got a letter in the mail that said that they were six months behind in their house payments, and the bank was going to have to foreclose on the house. She was shocked. She never saw the mail; he always picked it up. She thought he had been making house payments all along.

They made good money. So, where did the money go? She didn't know. I even tried to help them, but he cheated me out of $2,500. Twelve grown men should have gotten hold of him and carried him 12 miles out in the country and prayed for him for 12 hours!

I saw the wife a few years ago and asked her how her husband was doing. She said, "It's just hell on earth."

I spent hours talking to this man. He would do better for a few days and then just revert back to the same things he always did. He was a carnal Christian. His flesh was dominating him. All the bills were stacking up; they owed everyone. He would buy anything in the world. Even though he was behind on his house, if he saw a sport coat he liked, he would buy it. He should have had enough sense not to buy anything! He should have taken the money and paid his bills.

She definitely had more sense than he did. There's no doubt about that. I talked to both of them, and she was twice as smart as he was. That could have been part of the trouble. He was just using her because she was smarter than he was and made more money. He couldn't have made it on his own. But she should have been involved with the finances, too. It just wasn't right. So in the end, all their money was gone, and they still had unpaid bills. On top of all that, they lost their house. It's important to discuss financial matters before you get married.

#4 Children

The number four problem in marriages is children. Before my wife and I were married, we discussed how many children we wanted. But we also discussed how we wanted to discipline our children. I said to my wife, "I've been in so many preachers' homes where the parents were not in agreement. And the children learned that early. They would play one parent against the other one. I've seen three- and four-year-old children who had more sense than both their mother and father put together. People can lose their children because of things like that."

We also decided that we would never discuss another person's faults in front of our children. We agreed on this before we were ever married. You're going to cause your kids lots of problems if, as a pastor, you talk about all the deacons' faults. Your kids won't have any confidence in anyone.

So we never discussed other people's faults, including those of our church members. Our children always thought that all of our members were sprouting angels' wings! They didn't know that it was just their shoulder blades sticking out!

It's also important not to let your children hear you arguing about something in front of them, especially if you're arguing about them. Wait until you are by yourselves. If you think that your spouse is a little strict on the children, talk with him or her about these things. Realize that you have a life at stake—not only a physical life, but a spiritual life that could spend eternity in hell. And it's your responsibility to do the right thing by them as children!

I remember at one meeting I went to, I stayed with a young pastor. I was in my early thirties, and he was just slightly older than I was. His oldest boy was a few years older than my son Ken. I stayed in his home and had a chance to talk with him while I was there.

I could see some things that were not right in his home. First of all, he didn't treat his wife right. He was too self-ish. He was walking in the flesh more than he was walking in the Spirit. Second, he didn't treat his children right. And third, he couldn't control his temper. He would just fly off the handle at any little thing. If his wife or children crossed him the least little bit, he was liable to knock them down or slap them. Well, I know this much: If he can't control his temper, he can't control his physical appetite, either for food or for sex.

My custom at this time was to fast two days a week. I drank water, but didn't eat anything. When I would fast, I would fast unto the Lord. It was not something I shared with others; I just kept it to myself. But when I would stay at someone's home, they would notice that I was not eating.

This young pastor noticed I was fasting and said, "I can't fast. I've never been able to fast, even one meal." Unless a person has a medical condition, there's something wrong with someone who can't fast at least one meal. We should have some control over our appetites. Then in talking with him, I found out that he couldn't even go to a convention by himself, because he couldn't do without sex.

I could see what was happening. For one thing, he wasn't living right in front of his children. So I said, "You know, you're going to lose all of your children!"

Many people make the mistake of saying, "God promised this, and God said that. I believe God. I'm making the right confession." And they forget all about the way they are living. It doesn't matter how many right confessions you're making. If you're not living right, it's not going to work!

I pleaded with that dear brother; I was almost in tears. But he didn't do anything about it. His children grew up, and his oldest boy married. Unfortunately, his boy didn't know any other way to act except like his father.

Children not only inherit physical characteristics, but they also pick up on the personalities and behaviors of their parents. Have you ever tried to correct your own children? Many times you see yourself in them, because they have inherited your same characteristics. They act like you, and they look like you. They're your children!

So this oldest boy had a temper just like his father. When he got mad, he would slap his wife, and she would go to her parents' house. After three or four years of marriage, the same thing was still happening. They would be in church for a while, shouting the victory. Then they would be mad at each other, and neither one of them would go to church.

Because this boy couldn't control his temper, he couldn't control any of his physical appetites either—just like his daddy. His wife put up with it all she could, but, finally, she just left him, and moved back into her parents' house.

This boy thought about what his wife had done and decided to go to her parents' house. He thought, *I'm going to go over there and get her; that's what I'm going to do! After all, she's mine!* So about 10:00 p.m. one night, he went over there and started pounding on the door.

He said to his father-in-law, "I've come after my wife."

His father-in-law said, "She's not going!" His father-in-law didn't even open the door all the way; he just opened it a crack.

The husband said, "I will tear the door down if I have to. I've come after her, and I'm going to take her home. The Bible says that the husband is the head of the wife, and she's going to do what I tell her to do!"

While he was tearing the door down, his father-in-law got a shotgun and killed him. This is a sad story. But twenty years before that, I told this boy's father how his children were going to turn out. I tried to get him to make some changes, but he wouldn't listen.

If you don't conquer these things, you'll reap them in your own life, and you'll reap them in the lives of your children. If you can't conquer your temper, you won't be able to conquer your physical appetites—any of them! First Corinthians 9:27 says, *"But I keep under my body, and bring it into subjection: lest that by any means, when I have preached to others, I myself should be a castaway."*

CHAPTER SIX

Life in the Home

The law of love should govern our home life and every other part of our life. Let's read what Jesus said in the Gospel of John.

JOHN 13:34–35

34 *A new commandment I [Jesus] give unto you, That ye love one another; as I have loved you, that ye also love one another.*

35 *By this shall all men know that ye are my disciples, if ye have love one to another.*

Jesus had more to say about love in the Gospel of John chapter 14.

JOHN 14:15,21,23–24

15 *If ye love me [Jesus], keep my commandments. . . .*

21 *He that hath my commandments, and keepeth them, he it is that loveth me: and he that loveth*

> *me shall be loved of my Father, and I will love
> him, and will manifest myself to him. . . .*
>
> 23 *Jesus answered and said unto him, If a man love
> me, he will keep my words: and my Father will love
> him, and we will come unto him, and MAKE OUR
> ABODE WITH HIM.*
>
> 24 *He that loveth me not keepeth not my sayings: and
> the word which ye hear is not mine, but the
> Father's which sent me.*

Again in the Gospel of John, chapter 15, we see Jesus
emphasizing the law of love.

> **JOHN 15:10–12**
>
> 10 *If ye keep my commandments, ye shall abide in my
> love; even as I have kept my Father's command-
> ments, and abide in his love.*
>
> 11 *These things have I spoken unto you, that my joy
> might remain in you, and that your joy might be
> full.*
>
> 12 *This is my commandment, THAT YE LOVE ONE
> ANOTHER, AS I HAVE LOVED YOU.*

Jesus is making it very plain to us—we are to love one
another, as He has loved us! No one can do that except
born-again people. No one can do that except people who
are new creatures in Christ. An unregenerate person cannot
love like Christ loves. We have to have the love of God living
in us. Romans 5:5 says that the love of God has been shed
abroad in our hearts by the Holy Ghost. A born-again person can love like Christ loves!

> **EPHESIANS 5:2**
>
> 2 *And walk in love, as CHRIST ALSO HATH LOVED
> US, AND HATH GIVEN HIMSELF for us an offer-
> ing and a sacrifice to God for a sweet-smelling
> savour.*

Another translation says, "an offering and a sacrifice to
God, for an odor of sweet fragrance." Jesus gave Himself for

us as an offering and a sacrifice to God, for an odor of sweet fragrance. Because of His great love for us, we can love others.

All of these scriptures admonish us to walk in love, and to have the love law working itself out in our home life and in our marriages. We should be walking in divine love in every area of our lives, including our marriages.

The husband should give himself up for the wife, as Christ gave Himself up for the Church. And the wife should give herself up for her husband, as Christ also gave Himself up for the Church. That's really walking in love and keeping the Lord's commandments. As the husband and the wife give themselves to one another, they are laid on the altar of marriage. And the two become one in Christ, each living for and to bless the other.

The Atmosphere of the Home

Ephesians 5:22 and 23 says, *"Wives, submit yourselves unto your own husbands, as unto the Lord. For the husband is the head of the wife, even as Christ is the head of the church: and he is the saviour of the body."* The husband must take his place as the head of the woman in Christ, just as Christ is the head of the Church. Then the woman must take her place as the helpmeet as God planned it in the Garden of Eden. The wife assumes the responsibilities of the home. She is the queen of the home.

As we studied before in chapter 3, sometimes people take these verses in Ephesians very legalistically. They grasp the "letter of the law," but miss the spirit of it. They think that the husband is supposed to be the dictator of the home, ruling the wife and telling her what she is supposed to do. Another translation of Ephesians 5:22 says, *"Wives, walk in love with your husband, as Christ also walked in love toward you."* Doesn't that make more sense? The husband is the love-head of the wife, as Christ is the Love-Head of the

Church. Just as the Church is subject to Christ, so the wife is subject to her husband in everything.

All the heartaches, all the tears, all the sufferings of domestic life come out of the fountain of selfishness. But when both husband and wife surrender to the lordship of divine love, they are surrendering to God, because God is love. And God fills the home with love.

Remember, we read in the Gospel of John that Jesus said, "If you keep My commandment to love one another, My Father and I will come and make our home with you" (John 14:23; 15:10–12). Therefore, people coming into your home should be able to sense the Presence of God.

My aunt, my mother's only sister, was a secretary to the mayor of the city. And my uncle, my mother's only brother, was vice president of one of the banks of the city. Now my aunt and uncle didn't mind me preaching in the country as a Baptist preacher. But when I got hooked up with the "holy rollers and tongue-talkers" (that's what they called them back then), they said I was an embarrassment to the whole family.

I never said a word in retaliation; I just stayed kind and sweet and walked in love. I was led by God never to say a single word to any of my relatives about being saved. I never said one word to them! I never invited them to come and hear me preach or even to go to church.

Now you'll have to ascertain for yourself what to do in your own family, because each situation is different. I do believe that our greatest testimony is our actions.

I knew that when my relatives saw something real in me, they would all want it. And you know what? Every single one of them followed me in!

Now, that doesn't mean that we shouldn't vocally testify, but I think we should be wise about it. Some people are just blabbing off all the time and not living right. There's an old

Chinese proverb that says, "Your actions speak so loud, I can't hear what you're saying."

My aunt had said, "You'll never see me down there at that Full Gospel Tabernacle." But in the process of time, over a period of 11 years, my aunt said to my mother, "You know, there must be something to that baptism with the Holy Ghost and that speaking in tongues. I've observed over the years that Kenneth's children are never sick."

Now my children did have minor ailments every once in a while, but we would always get the victory over them. We never had any prolonged sickness in our home. My relatives were sick. And even other Full Gospel people were sick, because they had not learned how to walk in the fullness of what God had for them.

In 11 years of married life, my aunt never came to visit us. But by the time I was out in field ministry, she decided to come. After her visit, she said to my mother, "You know, going into that home was almost like going to Heaven. You could feel the Presence of God. I said that I would never go to that Full Gospel Tabernacle, but I'm going now." And she went.

If God is living in a place, a person should be able to sense His Presence. John 14:23 says, ". . . *we will come unto him, and make our abode with him.*" God the Father and Jesus will come and make their home with you. They will live with you! When both husband and wife surrender to the lordship of love, God fills the home.

The Power of Words

The home atmosphere is created by words. Words linger in the atmosphere long after people have departed.

One time, my wife and I were traveling in another state. We were on our way to begin a meeting. My wife said, "We ought to stop and see Brother and Sister So-and-so." They were pastors of a church we had held a meeting at about eleven months before.

I said, "I don't know. We're in a hurry." We had a service that night, and it was already afternoon. But since their parsonage was only about two blocks away from the freeway, I thought it wouldn't hurt to go by and greet them anyway.

So we just whipped off the freeway, and within a matter of a few seconds, we were at their house. We drove up the driveway and didn't see a car. The garage was closed. I said, "I don't think they're home. But I'll ring the doorbell anyway."

When I rang the doorbell, no one showed up. So I rang it again, and then I rang it a third time. About that time, I heard someone coming. I waited, and the pastor opened the door. He and his wife had been lying down taking a nap. So when he saw us, I said, "Don't let us disturb you."

He said, "We were resting. Come on in; my wife will want to see you. Just sit here in the living room, and we'll be out in just a moment."

So we sat down in the living room while he went to get his wife. Without either one of us saying anything to one another, we both noticed that sharp words had been spoken in the home. We noticed the exact same thing at the same time. We could feel it in the atmosphere.

If you can sense the Presence of God, you can sense other things as well. We learned later that they had had a disagreement that almost broke up their marriage. But thank God it was put back together.

Both the husband and the wife had not surrendered to the lordship of love. If love words had been spoken in the home, there would have been an atmosphere of love there instead of sharpness. If people could only learn that! If love is in the parents' words, then their children will be products of those love words.

So many times, we've had people say to us, "I have a teenager, and we can't do a thing in the world with him. He won't come to church and so on." People have thought we would understand their dilemma because we also had a teenage son. But our son wasn't like that at all. If he went somewhere, he would tell his mother where he was going and when he would be back. And he would be back at the time that he said. He wouldn't go off and leave his mother and sister late at night without seeing after them. He would stay home when he needed to study, and nothing could keep him from going to church.

You see, he was a gentleman. And the reason he was a gentleman was because I had been a gentleman in front of him. I knew he would follow in my footsteps. When your children are brought up in the nurture and admonition of the Lord, and you're walking with the Lord, they'll do the same. The Bible says, *"Train up a child in the way he should go: and when he is old, he will not depart from it"* (Prov. 22:6).

When Ken was a teenager, he noticed that many of the rebellious teenagers in his high school happened to be preacher's kids. He said to me, "Dad, I know exactly what the problem is. I talk to these pastor's sons."

Ken had just turned 16 and gotten his driver's license. And I had just purchased a new car. Since I was out preaching, Ken drove the new car from Texas to the West Coast with my wife and our daughter Pat. Some of the pastor's sons that Ken knew said, "You mean your daddy lets you drive?"

"Why," he said, "sure."

"Well, our daddy would never let us drive." You see, that's the reason why they turned out like they did. You have to put your confidence in your children. You have to build confidence in them.

Then they said, "You mean your daddy plays games with you?"

"Yeah, sure," he said.

"Oh, our daddy wouldn't even let us play games." That's the reason they went wild when they got out on their own.

"You mean your daddy gets out there and throws the football with you? He hits flies with a ball and a bat? And he catches them?"

"Well," he said, "yeah, sure."

"Our daddy wouldn't even let us play ball." That's why they turned out like they did. Their parents didn't have any time for them. Too many times, that's the reason why parents lose their kids.

When Ken graduated from high school, I sat him down and said, "Son, I've taught you what is right. Now you can go where you want to go and do what you want to do. You're 19 years old. If you don't know by now, then you'll never know." We still didn't have any problems. I don't mean that he was an angel and did everything perfectly. He made some mistakes and missed it, but he always came back to what he was taught.

Our children were never rebellious. They were kids, and you can't put a grown-up head on a kid. But the right words were spoken in the home. We walked in love toward one another. Our home was filled with the love of God. What a difference it makes! When both husband and wife surrender to the lordship of love, God fills the home.

Ephesians 5:28 through 30 leads us into the very heart of marriage itself.

EPHESIANS 5:28–30

> *28 So ought men to love their wives as their own bodies. He that loveth his wife loveth himself.*

29 *For no man ever yet hated his own flesh; but nour-isheth and cherisheth it, even as the Lord the church:*

30 *For we are members of his body, of his flesh, and of his bones.*

Paul uses the illustration of Christ and the Church again. The Church is the Body of Christ. Does Christ love His Body? The Lord loves His Body. He nourishes and cherishes it. So should the husband nourish and cherish his wife. The husband should love his wife as he loves his own body. He should cherish her body, as Christ cherishes His Body, the Church.

Set a Good Example for Your Children

Every home should be the temple of God. Jesus says, *". . . If a man love me, he will keep my words: and my Father will love him, and we will come unto him, and MAKE OUR ABODE WITH HIM"* (John 14:23). This is God's ideal for the Body of Christ! He wants to make His home with us.

Then the home where babies should be born into is the home of God. How sacred is the place where God's little ones live! Every child has a right to be born of a godly mother and to be born into a godly home.

Do wicked men and women have a right to bring inno-cent babies into a home where the child will be cursed by their parents' influence? Well, legally they do, but morally they don't.

Does a father have any right to gratify his own selfish desires in forming bad habits that will injure the children who are born to him, children who will one day follow in his footsteps? No, every father owes it to his children to walk with God! Look at Colossians 3:21: *"Fathers, provoke not your children to anger, lest they be discouraged."* We have a responsibility to our children.

Years ago, I heard this illustration, which is a true story. In the days of prohibition, a certain man had a still; he was making whiskey and selling it. He decided to go out to the barn to check up on it. It had been snowing, and the snow was deep.

He looked around, and his little boy who was about five years old was following him—walking right in his footsteps. He said, "Son, go on back. The snow's too deep for you."

"Oh," he said, "Daddy, I'm walking in your footsteps."

This man got under such conviction that he got saved and destroyed his still. He realized that his five-year-old boy was growing up, following in his footsteps.

That's the case most of the time. There are exceptions, of course, but the majority of the time, that's absolutely the case. Every father owes it to his children to walk with God. Again, Colossians 3:21 says for the father not to provoke his children to anger, or they'll be discouraged. God is talking to fathers who have brought babies into the world and then destroyed them with bad influences and bad examples.

Ephesians 6:4 says, *"And, ye fathers, provoke not your children to wrath: but bring them up in the nurture and admonition of the Lord."* Another translation says, "Nurture them in the sweet influence and admonitions of the Lord."

Many times I have had to ask Ken (even as a little boy) to forgive me. I have said to him, "I did wrong. Now what I did was right. I should have corrected you, but I did it in the wrong way. I got angry, and I'm sorry. I repent." It was important that I ask Ken to forgive me so that I would not provoke him to wrath. That's what Ephesians 6:4 means.

When children see the love law operating in their parents, they will walk in the light of it. I believe that's why we never had any major problems with our children.

I told you the story of my brother-in-law in chapter 1. He and my sister had two children. One night I was having a Bible study in someone's home and my brother-in-law decided to come. On our way back home from the Bible study, we started talking. I talked to him about his family. He listened and cried. Tears were running off his face.

I said, "Doc, you know, you have two small children, only nineteen months apart." Now I had witnessed to him about the Lord when the opportunity presented itself. I didn't push the subject; he would bring it up himself.

I said to him, "From a standpoint of just being a human being, I feel very deeply about this, because my home was broken. I was left an orphan boy, with no daddy, with no male role model in my life from the time I can remember until I was seventeen years old.

"No one ever gave me anything. My aunt one time gave me a nickel—one time in 17 years! I know what it means to suffer as a child, to go hungry, to be deprived. But I had enough get-up-and-go even in my weakened physical condition to drag myself out and pull weeds out of the neighbor's flower garden for 10 cents.

"My mother tried to carry the load for four children, but for years she was sick. And when my daddy left, she had a nervous breakdown. At the age of nine, I went to live with my grandmother. My grandmother loved me, but my aunt who was thirty years old was still living at home at the time. My aunt was jealous of me because she was used to getting all the attention, and so, she didn't show me any affection. I didn't know anything about natural love."

I told Doc, my brother-in-law, that he was following in my dad's footsteps—running around with women, drinking, and then gambling his money away. I said to him, "For the sake of your children, get your life right with God. I've been in your children's place, and I know the heartache and the hurt."

He would weep and weep; tears would fall down his face. But he still wouldn't change anything in his life. When his boy got to be nine years old, he began to regress instead of progress. Instead of growing up and looking like a nine-year-old, he began to look like he was about seven years old.

I tried my best to fight that thing. I fasted and prayed. I put in many hours trying to get healing for his boy. The Lord said to me, "The child's spirit is all right. But he has syphilis on the brain. He got it from his daddy." Eventually, the boy had to be put into the state home.

Some time later, my wife and I were attending a convention in the same town that the boy was in, and so, we went to see the boy. The superintendent of the home was also a medical doctor. He said to me, "Reverend, do you know what is wrong with the child?"

I said, "Yes, sir. I know."

He said, "The child has been here two years, but we just recently found out what is wrong with him."

He said, "Do you know?"

I said, "Yes, I know."

He said, "What's the matter with him?"

I said, "He has syphilis on his brain."

He said, "You're not a doctor; how did you know?"

I said, "The Spirit of God told me."

He said, "He must have, because we couldn't find out what was wrong with him for two years."

Then the doctor said, "You tell any of the family that if they want to see him, they better come and see him now, because he can't possibly live much longer."

I went back home and told those that were interested. As my wife and I were walking down the street, we saw his daddy. He was only thirty-seven years old at the time, but he was shaking all over like an old man. He stood there and wept. Neglected opportunity brings regret, both in the lives of sinners and Christians.

When he got close to us, he said, "Ken! Is that you?"

I said, "Yeah, it's me, Doc."

We were on the street. People were all around. And he began to cry, "Where's my boy? Do you know where he is?"

I said, "Yeah, I know where he is." Then I told him what the doctor said. "If you're going to see him, you'll have to go right away." He began to scream on the street! Oh, the torment of neglected opportunities!

"Is there anything I can do? Can I help my boy? Is there anything I can do for my boy?" he screamed.

"No," I said, "there's nothing you can do. You could have done something. You should have done something. I tried to get you to do something, but you wouldn't listen."

I remember when my children were born. When Ken was born, I took that little one in my hands and said, "Dear God, thank You for him. I realize that as I hold this little one in my hands, I hold life in my hands—not just a physical life, but a spirit. I know that I am responsible to train him well, to live right before him, and to set an example for him. I know that as a result of my training, he will either go to Heaven or hell when he dies." That's solemn thinking, but I knew what the Bible said. I had seen it with my daddy and with others. It was important for me to live right in front of my children.

I just always believed I could do what the Bible said I could do. I decided to train my children up in the nurture and the admonition of the Lord. The Bible says, *Train up a child in the way he should go: and when he is old, he will not depart from it* (Prov. 22:6).

Then I said, "This child will grow up strong, healthy, and without sickness and disease. He will develop alert mentally and stalwart spiritually. Amen."

He was only two-and-a-half hours old when I prayed that prayer. I never had to pray another prayer. In fact, I don't think I prayed a half dozen times for him.

I said the same thing to God when my daughter Pat was born. I pledged to do my part, to live right in front of her, and to walk in love. I told the Lord that I would bring her up in the nurture and admonition of the Lord. I never prayed that either one of my children would ever be saved. Why? I had already said it. I knew they would be. The thought never occurred to me that they might not be.

Now if I had gone off with some other woman and left them and lived like the devil, then I would have no right to claim anything. I would have forfeited my spiritual authority and my rights.

But both of my children got saved at an early age. Both of them were filled with the Holy Ghost. Of course, they were children. You can't put a grown-up head on a child. But we never had some of the problems that others had.

I believe in making the right confession. But you see, the right confession is not going to work unless I do this other first. That's where people miss it. They don't set the right laws in motion. They keep making confessions and nothing happens, because they're not living right. It won't work then.

I was twenty-two years old when Ken was born and was pastoring a church at the time. I predicted—not on the basis of revelation but on the basis of the knowledge of the Bible—how Ken would turn out. I also predicted how the babies who were born to people in my church would turn out. How did I do that? I watched to see if the parents were "doers" of the Word (James 1:22–26). Did they walk in the light of the Word?

Many were just "hearers" of the Word. They didn't walk in divine love in their home. And do you know what? I never missed it on any of them. When those children were all grown, my predictions were one hundred percent accurate. I predicted that if their parents kept living like they were and not walking in love—even though they were saved and Spirit-filled—their children would turn out the same way.

Children are the heritage of God in a home. When a child is born, the father and mother no longer belong to themselves. They are to live for this new life that their union has brought into being. The child is to reproduce the parents in his own life. There is to be a blending of the father's strength, love, and devotion to the mother and the mother's love, forbearance, and gentleness with the father, in this offspring of love. For children are spirit beings, and they are eternal.

Train Up Your Children

I remember that when I was only twenty-two years old, I taught a Bible class. Ken was just a few months old at the time. I taught a large class, made up of married couples aged 35 and older. An older gentleman who was around sixty-seven years old came up to me. He had two girls and one boy who were already grown and married. They had been gone from home for some time.

In the particular lesson I was teaching, the text was Proverbs 22:6—*"Train up a child in the way he should go: and when he is old, he will not depart from it."* This scripture is found in the Old Testament. And in the New Testament, we're told to bring our children up in the nurture and admonition of the Lord (Eph. 6:4).

Well, this man spoke up in class and said to me, "Brother Hagin, that old prophet or whoever it was that said to train up a child in the way that he should go and when he is old, he'll not depart from it, sure did miss it. Didn't he?"

I said, "What do you mean? Did the Bible miss it?"

He said, "You know, my wife and I taught our children what was right. We took them to church when they were small. But after they became teenagers, we told them what was right. And I'm reluctant to say this, but it's absolutely the truth: Both daughters became prostitutes, and the boy ended up in the penitentiary."

"Brother, first you ought to repent and ask God to forgive you, because that's not just some old prophet who said that; it's the Word of God that is saying to train up your child," I responded. "Now you said that you *told* them what was right. Do you know what the word 'train' means?

"When you were younger in your profession, you trained horses and sometimes you trained mules to work. Did you just tell those horses and mules that they ought to be out of the barn working? Did you tell them that they ought to be hitched to the plow? No, you made them do it! That doesn't mean that you were mean to the horses and mules. All you had to do was just pop the horse or mule by its ear and tell it what to do and it would get right over in place.

"You see, you don't have to be mean to children, but you do need to train them. But you didn't train your children. It's absolutely the truth!"

Well, I'm glad to say that his oldest daughter came to visit, and they got her to come to church. And she and the man she was living with got saved, and then, they got married. People who are saved should not live together without being married. There may be people who are doing it, but they are not in fellowship with God. If they were saved, then they've backslidden. But thank God that this man's daughter and the man she was living with got saved, filled with the Holy Ghost, and turned out to be wonderful Christians.

God has a way of helping us anyway, even when we miss it. If the Bible says that I am to train up a child in the way he should go, then I can do that. If the Bible says for me to do something, I can do it. Now you train children by setting

the right example in front of them—by living right in front
of them.

One time Ken got a new bicycle, and he learned to ride
it. In fact, he would get on it and go like crazy. I told him
that if he didn't watch it, he would run into something.
And it wouldn't be my fault or anyone else's, because he
wouldn't have been paying attention to what he was doing.

So one day, he was coming down the road real lickity
split, and one of the high school football players went by on
the highway in front of the church. This football player was
racking his bike. Ken was in the second grade at the time,
and he thought the high school players were really something. He turned around to wave at the football player, and
all of a sudden hit the back end of the bus I was driving.

You see, I had confessed the Word over him—that he
would be protected. But he had to do something in the natural; he had to look where he was going while he was riding
that bicycle. So it works hand in hand. I can confess and
believe God, but there is a part to play in the natural as well.

The same is true in regard to a child defending himself.
I've always taught Ken not to start anything. If he did, if
he started it, then I would deal with him. But if someone
jumped on him, then that's a different story. I told Ken,
"Son, if you start the fight, I'm going to punish you. But
if someone else starts a fight with you, you have a right to
defend yourself. I don't believe that the Bible teaches that
you have to be a doormat for anyone to run over you, just
because you're a Christian."

I remember one situation when Ken was in the army.
He would stay in on Saturday evening and clean up around
his bunk and get it all nice and clean so that he could leave
early on Sunday morning and go into town to church. He
would stay with some friends in the church and not get
back until Sunday night. The rest of the guys caroused on

Saturday night and stayed in on Sunday night to clean up their area and get it all ready.

For four Sundays in a row, Ken came in on Sunday night and found the guys all around his bunk, playing cards, drinking their beer, and so on. He would spend half the night getting his area ready for inspection the next morning. So one Sunday night he came in after about four weeks of putting up with that and said, "I'm going to the day room to get a coke. When I get back, you all had better have this mess cleaned up."

When Ken got back, they hadn't cleaned up his area. He walked in, braced his legs against the bunk, and grabbed hold of it. Then he threw it over about three or four of them. He backed against the wall, as about eight of them came after him. About that time, four other guys who were trying to sleep jumped out of their bunks and said, "We wondered how long the preacher was going to put up with that nonsense. There are five of us and eight of you all. The odds are about even. Come on, if you want to get it on."

After that, the guys who had given Ken so many problems said, "Well, the preacher will turn his cheek and take it like the Bible says. But after that, he does something about it." And that's just the way I taught my son to do it. I taught him not to be obnoxious and fight people. But if he has no other choice and they want to jump on him, I believe that he has every right to defend himself.

Jesus taught this when He went into the temple and defended it. I don't think He had words that were syrupy sweet when he picked up that whip and drove those people out of the temple. I think His tongue was a little bit sharp. And I imagine that His eyes were popping out a little bit. He was upset that they were defiling His Father's house.

Now children will wrestle around and be mad at each other one minute. And the next minute, they'll be right back playing together. And I've noticed something else: If children find one that just lies down without defending himself, everyone jumps on him and he becomes the kicking post. I don't think that a child has to put up with that. I think that children can be Christians and still stand up for themselves.

When I first accepted the pastorate of a Full Gospel Church in the blacklands of north central Texas in 1939, there were two fellows who came to my church. Those were depression days, and times were hard. So those two fellows would go down to east Texas and buy handles from a factory that made hammer handles, ax handles, pick handles, and shovel handles. They would invest between twenty-five and fifty dollars a month. That doesn't sound like a lot of money now, but it was a whole month's salary back then.

Then they would peddle the handles out. On a particular occasion, they had just returned from east Texas with a load of handles. They put them in the back of a pick-up truck. They stopped at one of their houses to spend the night. They were both sleeping in the same room, but separate beds, you know. And it began to rain. It was pouring down, and one of them said to the other, "We have to get up and cover those handles."

The handles were made of wood, a green wood, and sometimes when the hot sun came out in the morning, they would warp. Then they weren't any good. They would have to be thrown out. Someone might say, "Oh the Lord will take care of the handles. I'm a believer." Well, that one load did exactly what the fellow said. All of them were warped. The Lord *didn't* take care of them. You see, you have to have enough sense to do something yourself!

The Responsibility of Parents

In the last church I pastored, there was a family who had just gotten back to church. They'd been out of church for years. The father came to the altar, got back in fellowship with God, and was filled with the Holy Spirit.

Their youngest daughter was 11 years old. That little girl never developed right. She was small, like a seven-year-old, and it seemed that she also had the mentality of a seven-year-old. In fact, she played with our little girl who was seven years old. This little girl was a slow learner and couldn't make it in school. But she got saved and filled with the Holy Spirit. And it seemed like her mentality increased. She was a very sweet girl.

Well, we resigned and left the church. About three years later, they had to put this little girl in the hospital in Dallas. They wanted us to come and pray for her. She was under an oxygen tent and in a coma. The doctors thought that she had a tumor on the brain. They said she wasn't going to live much longer.

So I prayed. Then my wife and I went to our meeting. But they called us again because the girl took a turn for the worse. So we prayed again.

We finally closed the meeting and drove home. When we got home, our phone was ringing. They wanted us to come to the hospital in Dallas and lay hands on this girl.

I went to the hospital and pulled the girl's oxygen tent up. I laid my hand on her forehead and started praying.

While my eyes were shut, I felt a warm hand on my hand, so I just took my hand off her head. I thought that maybe I was pressing too hard. I thought that maybe her mother took my hand off her forehead. So I shut my eyes again and put my hand back on her. Again, I felt that warm hand. So the third time I kept my eyes open. I felt the warm hand, but I couldn't see any hand.

I said to the Lord, "Why did you take my hand off her head?"

He said, "Because she's going to die."

"Lord," I said, "she loves you. I saw her when she got born again and filled with the Holy Spirit. Why is she going to die?"

He said, "She has one kidney about the size of an English pea, and the other kidney is only about half the size it should be. She doesn't have a tumor. She has functioned all her life with only half a kidney. Finally, this poison has spread all over her body and poisoned her brain. That's why she's in a coma."

"Well, couldn't You heal her?" I asked.

He said, "Her parents should have done something about it before she was born. While her mother was carrying her for nine months, her father left the church because he didn't like something that the pastor said. He backslid and wherever he went, he cussed the pastor. And her mother was running around spreading gossip about everyone in the church, instead of praying for her child. They opened the door for the devil. Just let the child come on Home. I want to take care of her."

The husband and wife were spiritually responsible. They didn't have to backslide and speak badly about the pastor. They were not going to get their prayers answered if they were cussing out a preacher. They were not going to get their prayers answered if they were running around spreading gossip. They should have been praying for that child. They should have been praying that every organ, cell, and tissue would develop normally and that she would be perfect physically.

Parents should have the best interests of their children at heart. Ephesians 6:1 says, *"Children, obey your parents in the Lord: for this is right."* I know some children who got saved, but their parents weren't Christians. Their parents forbid them to go to church. That doesn't mean the children should obey their parents if they are told to do things that are sinful and wrong.

Notice Paul says, "in the Lord." Children should obey their parents *in the Lord.* And walking in love is fulfilling all the promises of God. You can then receive the benefits of the promises. Let's look at the next two verses in Ephesians.

EPHESIANS 6:2–3

2 *Honour thy father and mother; which is the first commandment with promise;*

3 *That it may be well with thee, and THOU MAYEST LIVE LONG ON THE EARTH.*

The benefit or promise from walking in love is long life! Paul is saying that if you do this, you can know healing and health. When I would discipline our children, I would always read them this scripture.

I would say to Ken, "Son, I'm not reprimanding you or disciplining you because I want to. I don't get anything out of it. I have your interest at heart. I want you to be well. I don't want you to wind up in a hospital. I don't want you to die prematurely. I want you to live a long time on the earth."

If one of my children did something wrong, I would say, "If you do that, I'm going to punish you." Then I would keep my word. I never went back on my word. Now I was not punishing them every day. I wasn't even punishing them once a year. I probably only spanked Ken three or four times in his whole life.

I remember when Ken was only six years old. I told him early in the day to empty the wastebasket. At night we always prayed with our children and read the Word with them. When they were small before they ever started school, we read them Bible stories from a book written especially for children. We didn't read the *King James Version* of the Bible to them then because they didn't understand that. But we would read a Bible story every night and pray with them before they went to bed.

So this particular night, after we prayed, my wife and Pat went to bed. I usually had a bookcase of books and a desk in the living room. When they would go to bed about 10:00 p.m., I would go in the living room to read and study all night long.

Ken got out of bed, and he was crying. He said, "Daddy, I want you to forgive me."

I said, "What for?"

"Well," he said, "I disobeyed you. I didn't empty the wastebasket that you told me to." I saw the empty wastebasket and thought that he had emptied it, but I guess my wife did.

He said, "Where is that scripture that talks about not being sick and living a long time?" So I read it to him. And he said, "Well, I want to live a long time. I want you to forgive me."

I said, "Well sure, I forgive you. But let's get down here and pray and the Lord will forgive you." I didn't punish him. I didn't tell him I was going to punish him if he didn't empty the wastebasket. I said all that to show you how tender his heart was at only six years old. It was my responsibility as a parent to teach him. Ephesians 6:4 says to bring up our children in the sweet influence and admonitions of the Lord.

When my father-in-law passed away, I knew two years ahead of time that he was going to die. The Lord showed me, so I began to prepare my wife. She was the only daughter they had, and she was the baby of the family. She was daddy's girl. I knew it would be hard on her, so I began to talk to her. I began to say things like, "Honey, you know, your daddy is getting older. He's not going to live here forever."

Her father only had one son, and I remember that when he was dying, he called his son up to his bedside. I stood there at the foot of the bed. He held his son's hand and said, "Son, did your daddy ever mistreat you?"

He said, "No, sir."

"Did you ever hear your daddy curse?"

"No, sir."

"Did you ever hear him say a bad word?"

"No, sir."

"Did you ever hear him tell a vulgar joke?"

"No, sir."

"Son," he said, "have I ever failed to set the right example in front of you?"

He said, "No, sir."

I don't know what else he said to him, but I was overcome. I felt at a loss. My daddy left when I was six years old. I had to go to the bathroom and cry. I couldn't take it. I went to the bathroom and cried my heart out. I saw that I had missed so much. I learned later that the father also said, "Son, I want you to meet me over there." His son wasn't right with God at that time.

I thought about everything he said. I decided that when I come to the end of life's journey, I want to be able to say to my son, "Did I ever set the wrong example in front of you? Did you ever hear me say anything that was wrong? Did you ever hear me use foul language?" That was the most beautiful sight I had ever seen in my life. That grown young man was holding his daddy's hand in his. I'm glad I assumed my responsibility.

Children Who Are Already Grown

Many parents are placed in a situation where they are born again late in life, and their children are already 16 or 17 years old. If a child is already grown, how do you deal with that child? I have had some experience along that line.

When my niece was 15 years old, she came to live with us. My sister's husband had left her with five children to take care of, and we wanted to help.

I said to my niece, "Now, you know I'm a pastor of a church first. And there are some things that you've been doing and some ways that you've been dressing that you just can't do anymore, because people will think you're the pastor's daughter." I didn't try to put any pressure on her to make her do anything. I talked to her and explained that under the circumstances, there are some things she just couldn't do.

Then I endeavored to put confidence in her—just like I had with my own children. There were times we had to ground her, but she eventually got saved and filled with the Holy Spirit.

We would pray as a family every morning. She was in high school, and my kids were in grade school. Now I didn't ask her to pray. I would say, "You'll just have to wait because we always pray and read a chapter of the Bible before school." She would stand by the door. I didn't try to force her into anything. I didn't even invite her to pray.

So after a while, she got to where she would sit down with us. She wouldn't kneel, but she would sit down while we read the Bible and then prayed. She would just sit there. And after a while, she would kneel and pray. We never asked her to. Then soon after, she was saved and filled with the Holy Spirit.

When children are older, you'll have to exercise your faith, surround them with faith, and make them realize that as long as they're living at home, there are certain rules and regulations that they have to abide by. And you'll find that even at that age, they'll still respond to a little discipline. You don't have the opportunity that you had when they were younger, but it will still work!

A Mother's Request

At a Full Gospel Business Men's Convention in a certain large city, a lady came up to me after one of the afternoon teaching sessions. She said, "Brother Hagin, I want you to promise me something."

I said, "Well, I want to find out what it is first."

She said, "I want you to promise me you'll pray every day for my son. He's 15 years old, and I can't do a thing in the world with him. I can't get him to go to church. He's in with a gang and I'm afraid they're on drugs. He's out until three and four in the morning. I lie awake nights waiting for the phone to ring telling me they have him down at the jail."

I interrupted her before she could tell any more about how bad it all was. I said to her, "I'm not going to do it."

"You're not going to do what?" she asked.

"I'm not going to pray for him, much less pray every day," I responded.

That surprised her. She said, "You're not?"

"No ma'am. I'm not. I won't promise you I'll pray for him at all. You see, in the first place it wouldn't do any good, because you would nullify all the effects by your wrong believing and your wrong talking. No matter how many people pray, as long as you keep telling him that he'll never amount to anything, he'll wind up in reform school. He'll go to the penitentiary; he'll never make it."

Her eyes got big. She said, "How did you know I was talking that way to him?"

I said, "To be in the mess he's in, you had to talk him into it." We're products of words. Children are products of words. Words will make a boy love an education. Words will make a boy want to go to church, or they'll keep him out of church.

"What am I going to do?" she asked.

144

I explained, "Since you've gone so long this way and because he's as old as he is, just leave him alone. He resents your talking to him and trying to tell him anything. Just leave him alone. Don't tell him anything. Don't preach at him. Don't nag him.

"And then," I said, "change your thinking and change your talking. At home, even when you don't know where he is, say, 'I surround him with faith.' You have been surrounding him with doubt—now surround him with faith. And even if your heart doesn't believe it to begin with, say it out of your head, and your heart will start believing, 'I do not believe he's going to the reform school. I do not believe he's going to the penitentiary. I believe he's coming to God. I believe!' State what you believe."

"Well," she said, "I'll try it."

I told her, "It won't work. It won't work if you *try* it. But it will work if you'll *do* it. Jesus didn't say he would have whatever he *tried*. He said he would have whatever he *says*."

That convention was in August. The Full Gospel Business Men had another convention in that same city the next year in October, 14 months later, and I was back again to speak.

After the afternoon service a lady came up to me and said, "Brother Hagin, do you remember me?"

"No, I meet so many people that I don't really remember you."

"Oh," she said. "Do you remember when you were here a year ago and I ran up and asked you to pray for my boy and you shocked me by saying you wouldn't?

"I want to tell you one thing. That works! Now, it didn't look like it was going to work. He got worse. And it was the hardest thing I ever did, keeping my mouth shut. But I kept saying—every day I said it, every night I said it—'I surround him with faith. I believe he's coming to God. I believe things are going to work out right in his life. I believe he's not going

145

to reform school.' My head said that was where he was going because of the bunch he was in with, but I said from my heart, 'He's not going to the reform school. I do not believe he'll wind up in the penitentiary.'"

She went on, "We went along that way for nearly a year, 10 months or so. Then one Sunday morning, after he'd been out nearly all night, he got up. Ordinarily he would be sleeping, but he got up and came to the breakfast table. [She was a widow.] And while we were eating, he said, 'Momma, I believe I'll go to Sunday school with you this morning.'"

She said, "I just acted nonchalantly and said, 'Now son, you were up awfully late, you probably need your rest.'" (Before she'd been nagging him to go.)

"No," he said, "I want to go."

"Well," she said, "it's up to you, but you only got a few hours sleep."

"I want to go," he said. And he went to Sunday school and stayed for church.

"The very next Sunday morning," she told me, "he was out until four in the morning, but again he was up for breakfast."

"Momma," he said to her, "I believe I'll go to Sunday school with you this morning."

She said, "Son, you were out late last night. You need your rest, you know."

"Well, yes," he said, "but I can go. I'm going."

He went to Sunday school, stayed for church, and that evening he said to her, "I believe I'll go back with you tonight." When the invitation was given, he went to the altar and was saved.

"Since then," she told me, "he's been filled with the Spirit. Now then, just like he was all out for the devil, he's all out for God. He's on fire for God! I believe he's going to turn into a preacher! I'll tell you, he's just a brand-new boy. I've got a brand-new boy.

"Thank you," she said. "At first I almost got my feelings hurt because you were so point blank with me. But I saw it. I corrected myself, and thank God, I've got a brand-new son."

"You know," she said, "I'll tell you something else. He's got a brand-new Momma."

She'd been saved and filled with the Holy Spirit and in a Full Gospel church for years, but she told me that day, "I don't think like I used to think. I almost pinch myself sometimes and say, 'Is this really me?' I used to worry, worry, worry, worry. Now I don't worry anymore.

"Not only that," she went on, "I feel so good physically, I feel like a young girl. I've got vim, vigor, and vitality." When she began to say the right thing, it worked for her. Jesus said, ". . . he shall have whatsoever he saith" (Mark 11:23).

Forgiveness

Colossians chapter 3 explains the law of love and the importance of forgiveness. If you have a quarrel with your spouse, you should forgive him or her, just as you would anyone else.

COLOSSIANS 3:1–25

1   *If ye then be risen with Christ, seek those things which are above, where Christ sitteth on the right hand of God.*

2   *Set your affection on things above, not on things on the earth.*

3   *For ye are dead, and your life is hid with Christ in God.*

4   *When Christ, who is our life, shall appear, then shall ye also appear with him in glory.*

5   *Mortify therefore your members which are upon the earth; fornication, uncleanness, inordinate affection,*

evil concupiscence, and covetousness, which is idolatry:

6   *For which things' sake the wrath of God cometh on the children of disobedience:*

7   *In the which ye also walked some time, when ye lived in them.*

8   *But now ye also put off all these; anger, wrath, malice, blasphemy, filthy communication out of your mouth.*

9   *Lie not one to another, seeing that ye have put off the old man with his deeds;*

10   *And have put on the new man, which is renewed in knowledge after the image of him that created him:*

11   *Where there is neither Greek nor Jew, circumcision nor uncircumcision, Barbarian, Scythian, bond nor free: but Christ is all, and in all.*

12   *Put on therefore, as the elect of God, holy and beloved, bowels of mercies, kindness, humbleness of mind, meekness, longsuffering;*

13   *FORBEARING ONE ANOTHER, AND FORGIVING ONE ANOTHER, if any man have a quarrel against any: even as Christ forgave you, so also do ye.*

14   *And above all these things put on charity, which is the bond of perfectness.*

15   *And let the peace of God rule in your hearts, to the which also ye are called in one body; and be ye thankful.*

16   *Let the word of Christ dwell in you richly in all wisdom; teaching and admonishing one another in psalms and hymns and spiritual songs, singing with grace in your hearts to the Lord.*

17   *And whatsoever ye do in word or deed, do all in the name of the Lord Jesus, giving thanks to God and the Father by him.*

18 *Wives, submit yourselves unto your own husbands, as it is fit in the Lord.*

19 *Husbands, love your wives, and be not bitter against them.*

20 *Children, obey your parents in all things: for this is well pleasing unto the Lord.*

21 *Fathers, provoke not your children to anger, lest they be discouraged.*

22 *Servants, obey in all things your masters according to the flesh; not with eyeservice, as menpleasers; but in singleness of heart, fearing God:*

23 *And whatsoever ye do, do it heartily, as to the Lord, and not unto men;*

24 *Knowing that of the Lord ye shall receive the reward of the inheritance: for ye serve the Lord Christ.*

25 *But he that doeth wrong shall receive for the wrong which he hath done: and there is no respect of persons.*

When you choose to forgive, love fills your home. When you and your spouse surrender yourselves to the law of love, you both are surrendering to God. And God fills your home with love.

No matter what has happened in the past, you can walk in the light of God's Word. You can create an atmosphere of love and acceptance by filling your home with words of love. Your children will be affected and all those who come into your home will sense the Presence of God.